MEDITERRANEAN ORNAMENTAL FLORA
GROUND COVERING AND CARPETING PLANTS

Xavier Bellido

ENGLISH VERSION
Alex Bramwell

Editorial Rueda, S. L.

Porto Cristo, 13
28924 Alcorcón (Madrid)
Tel. (91) 619 27 79 - Fax. (91) 610 28 55

Fotographs: Xavier Bellido

I.S.B.N.:84-7207-108-1
Depósito Legal B.: 30.076-1998
Imprime: EGEDSA, Sabadell, España

CONTENTS

TRAILING AND HANGING PLANTS WHICH CAN BE USED
AS GROUND COVER

Anredera cordifolia
Asparagus sprengeri
Bignonia capensis
Bougainvillea
Carissa grandiflora
Cissus antarctica
Cissus rhombifolia
Coprosma x kirkii 'Variegata'
Ficus repens
Hedera
Ipomoea acuminata
Lantana montevidensis
Leptospermum scoparium

Lonicera japonica
Lotus berthelotii
Pelargonium peltatum
Plectranthus australis
Rosmarinus lavandulaceus
Senecio angulatus
Smilax aspera
Streptosolen jamesonii
Trachelospermum jasminoides
Vinca major

SYMBOLS

Symbols	*Significance*
Mexico (example)	Country or area of origin
L, M, R	Rate of growth, slow, moderate, fast
PERENNE / H. CADUCA / SEMPERENNE	Leaves: evergreen, deciduous, semideciduous (1)
VI/VIII (example)	Months of flowering
FLOR PERFUMADA	Flowers perfumed
PLENO SOL / TOLERA LA SOMBRA / SOMBRA	Full sun, half-shade or shade, respectively
TOLERA LA CAL / SÓLO SUELO ÁCIDO	Grade of soil, basic or acidic
-5°C. (example)	Minimum temperature (if no figure then the plant resists -10° C. (2)
SOPORTA LA PROXIMIDAD DEL MAR	Thrives near the sea
MELIFERA	Honey producer, or visited by bees
TOLERA LA CONTAMINACIÓN DEL AIRE	Tolerates atmospheric contamination

(1) Semideciduous leaves are those which are only persistent in mild climates with relatively frost-free Winters.
(2) The minimum temperature resistance is valid if the cold comes on gradually, because sudden frosts, especially when out of season can damage even the most resistant plants.

INTRODUCTION

FLORA AND CLIMATE

You have in your hands a selection of the best and most interesting cover and carpeting plants that can be found or cultivated in Mediterranean climates, many of them are of subtropical origin.

The Mediterranean climate is characterised by short Springs and abrupt, dry, hot Summers, long, pleasant Autumns and mild sunny Winters with a wide range of temperature from night to day. There is a notable period of Summer drought, differing from the Autumn which is usually a rainy season taken advantage of by many species to flower or reflower as if it were a second Spring.

On describing some of the species the fire-proof value is indicated. This is a highly appreciated quality for stopping the advance of flames in zones exposed to forest fires.

ON THE TECHNICAL NAMES

Given that the scientific names vary with excessive frequency, increasing the number of synonyms and feeding the confusion, I have given preference to, not the most fashionable ones, but those that are most commonly used by horticulturists, gardeners and amateurs, as they are more descriptive and, therefore, easier to remember. Under equal conditions I have opted for those which are most easily written. It is clear that no synonym or alternative name can become antiquated as it always has equivalent value.

COMMON NAMES

Where these exist, I have selected the most commonly used and most descriptive including some South American ones which are very expressive and interesting.

GROUND COVER AND CARPETING PLANTS

These are the most likely to prosper covering the ground, some forming compact carpets, others cushions of variable height or those creeping or trailing shrubs and bushes which form ground-covering masses.

They should have perennial, evergreen leaves (although there are some exceptions) of sufficient vigour and density to prevent the development of weeds and should not require regular mowing in the case of carpeting species.

WHY DO THEY COVER ?

The Mediterranean ground-cover plants, from hot or dry regions cover the soil to maintain humidity and thus survive. Others also seek the warmth of the earth. Some trail along the ground because they cannot hang or cannot find the support they need to climb. Yet others creep looking for the shade and humidity beneath the trees.

THE ART OF COVERING THE GROUND

The popularity of xero-gardening (gardening with the maximum saving of water) is understandable as water is extremely scarce in many Mediterranean Gardens. Cover plants are ideal for this. Between ground cover and carpeting plants the vegetable tapestry of the garden can be completed.

AESTHETIC AND PRACTICAL ADVANTAGES

Cover plants are useful and economical because :
-They permit the replacement of typical water-consuming grass lawns
-They can provide flower cover and lawns of variegated foliage
- They permit the covering of difficult slopes and unmowable areas
- They help to frame flowerbeds, paths and steps
-They help to maintain humidity in the ground, thus benefiting other plants
-They prevent erosion during rainstorms
-They fix soil and consolidate slopes
-They help save water and labour in the garden
-They allow the creation of landscapes adapted aesthetically to the local, regional environment.

Definitively, they are plants of seductive beauty and diversity which permit us to enjoy the pleasures of the garden instead of having to continually wrestle with the problems of the climate.

Xavier Bellido

General Index

INDEX OF SCIENTIFIC NAMES

X

INDEX TO COMMON NAMES

Mediterranean climate zones

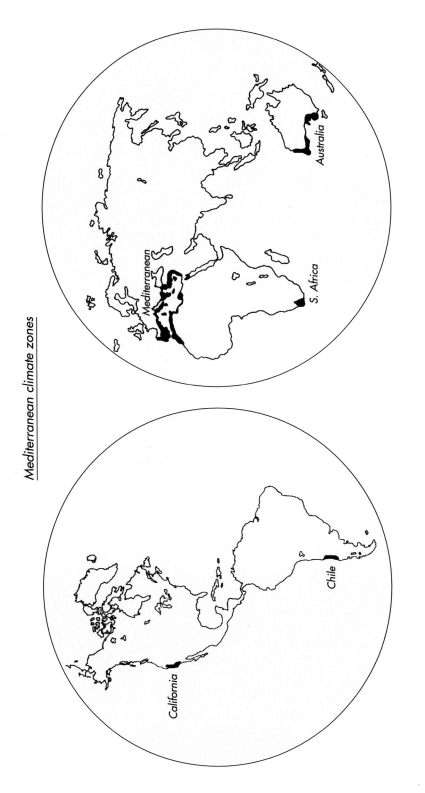

1. *ABELIA x GRANDIFLORA* 'Prostrata'
(Abelia rupestris grandiflora 'Prostrata')

China - M VI/X

Glossy Abelia

Hybrid (*A.chinensis* x *A. uniflora*).An attractive laxly branched, ground-covering bush growing up to 70cm.Its small bright green leaves take on beautiful bronze and purple tones in Autumn. The small white or pink bell-shaped flowers are abundant and long lasting. Their scent attracts butterflies.

Thrives in any well drained soil and is drought resistant although occasional summer watering improves its overall aspect and flowering capacity.

An interesting cover plant for walls and rockeries which is also suitable for containers.

Benefits from light, cosmetic pruning after flowering and if necessary, a heavy cut back at the end of winter. Cuttings should be taken in September.

SP. Abelia FR. Abélia GER. Abelie IT. Abelia

2. *ACANTHUS MOLLIS*

SE.Europe - R VI/VII   (-7°C.) ✓

Bear's Breech

A vigorous herbaceous plant of great ornamental value for its large, decorative leaves and spectacular, abundant, long lasting tubular flowers. The tall flower spikes are white or pink with lilac tinges and suitable for drying. The glossy leaves are lost at the end of Summer and return in the Autumn. Drought resistant and tolerant of both sun and shade. Soil can be of poor quality but must be cool.

The *A. mollis* latifolius form in the photograph is the most widely cultivated form of its species due to its large size and vigorous growth.

Forms excellent cover for dry areas beneath trees, rustic corners and semi-wild gardens.Beautiful combined with rock or in groups close to grass. Planting density 3/ m2. Suitable for containers.

The leaves should be cut to ground level after flowering. Propagation by division in October or March after pruning or by root cuttings in Autumn. The fruit make a characteristic sound when they scatter. Much appreciated by snails!

SP Acanto FR. Acanthe GER. Bärenklau IT. Branca ursina

3. *AEONIUM ARBOREUM* 'Schwarzkopf'
(Sempervivum arboreum 'Schwarzkopf')

Marocco - L II/III -   - (-3°C.) -

Black tree Aeonium

Very showy and ornamental variety. Long lived succulent with straight, upright branches crowned with rosettes of shiny, dark purple,(almost black) spathulate leaves. Forms bushes up to 1m. high. Produces lightly perfumed, golden yellow, conical inflorescences some 30cm. tall on 2-3 year old branches which then die.

Undemanding. Accepts light shade, although this affects its colouration, and a certain degree of humidity. Requires porous soil.

Very beautiful in groups, where it contrasts with the green, grey or yellow of other plants. Also close to pink (geraniums etc.) or yellow flowers (*Sedum praealtum*, etc.). Suitable for pots.

In May, cuttings from branches, rosettes or adult leaves can be taken and any tall or withered branches must be pruned to keep the plant low and compact. Occasional watering during dry periods prevents overgrowth.

SP. Siempreviva arbórea   FR. - GER. - IT.: *Aeonium arboreum*

4. *AGAPANTHUS UMBELLATUS*
(Agapanthus africanus, Crinum africanum)

S. Africa - L - [PERENNE] - VII/IX - [PLENO SOL] [TOLERA LA SOMBRA] [TOLERA LA CAL] (-7°C·) [TOLERA LA CONTAMINACIÓN DEL AIRE]

Blue African-lily

Very ornamental. Tuberous roots produce colonies of various individuals with straplike leaves and umbels of 20-30 spectacular intense blue flowers. Interesting because it flowers well in half-shade.Fairly undemanding:flourishes in any fertile and well drained soil. The *multiflorus* variety is the most widely cultivated for its large leaves and umbels of 40-60 brilliant blue flowers. The «Albidus» variety has white flowers.

Useful for lightly shaded positions for example under trees and as ground cover in reduced spaces. Lovely alongside rock, close to a pond, combined with Amaryllis Belladonna or with a backround of oleanders, *Lantana camara* and *Hypericum* x «Hidcote». Suitable for containers.

Watering is needed during flowering but humidity must be avoided during the winter resting period. Plants can be divided in September every 6-7 years. The leaves are lost at -8°C but the plant survives down to-15°C. The roots have medicinal value.

SP. Agapanto, tuberosa Fr. Agapanthe GER. Afrikcanische liebesblume

IT. Agapanto.

5. *AGATHAEA COELESTIS*
(Felicia amelloides, Aster rotundifolius)

S.Africa - R - [PERENNE] - V/X - [PLENO SOL] [TOLERA LA CAL] - (-5°C.)

Blue daisy

Charming, rounded, creeping or hanging shrublet that can grow up to 60cm tall, with small, greyish, finely hispid oval leaves. Its numerous flowers resemble small daisies with delightful, rounded, sky blue ligules. Often confused with the similar species *Felicia amoena.*

Varieties with variegated leaves, white flowers and a giant form with bright blue flowers exist. Resistant to drought but benefits from occasional summer waterings.

Excellent cover plant for small surfaces, slopes, rock gardens and for hanging on walls along with other striking cover plants (Verbenas, Mesems, *Senecio saxifraga* etc.). Suitable for potting.

A low maintenance plant that can easily be reproduced from cuttings taken in Autumn or Spring.

SP. Agatea, Celestina FR. Paquerette bleue   GER. - IT. *Agathaea coelestis*

6.   *AJUGA REPTANS*

Europe - R -  - IV/V -

Bugle weed, Carpet bugle

A very prolific, highly ornamental, creeping plant that forms excellent ground cover in shaded areas. Produces numerous stolons which root easily. Its lustrous leaves are 5-10cm. long and the blue or white flower spikes are fairly decorative. Can be used to replace grass under trees as it does not need mowing. Very vigorous and will thrive anywhere cool. There are lovely varieties: «*Atropurpurea*», with bronze foliage, «*Variegata*» and «Tricolor»,with green and cream and red, pink and yellow variegation respectively. These last two require sunlight to maintain their colouration

A carpeting plant that is very useful as a natural weed regulator for both large and small areas. Requires regular watering during the Summer.

Can be divided and planted at any time. Widely used to treat diarrhoea and haemorrhages as its high tannin content gives it astringent properties.

SP. Consuelda media, Búgula, Lechuguilla   FR. Bugle rampante

GER. Kriechender günsel   IT. Bugala

7. *ALOE CILIARIS*

S.Africa - L -  - II/IV - - (-3°c.) -

Climbing Aloe

Succulent, spreading shrub with half-woody, slender stems which are branched and up to 5 m. long. They are clothed from top to bottom with spirally arranged, succulent leaves about 15 cm. long with finely toothed margins.

In Winter and Spring numerous attractive inflorescences appear, these reach 20-25 cm. in height and are full of nodding tubular scarlet flowers with yellow-tinged tips. Flowering continues intermittently during the rest of the year.

It prospers in any type of soil including calcareous and is very drought resistant. It is a good ground cover with time for rockeries and dry slopes. It is used in massive plantings as a fire-break. This species is easily propagated by cuttings taken in April-May.

SP.- FR.- GER.- IT.: *Aloe ciliaris.*

8. *ALYSSUM SAXATILE (Aurinia saxatilis)*

Europe - M -  - IV/V -

Basket of gold

Vigorous herbaceous plant with greyish leaves and branches up to 30cm high that sometimes lignify. Golden yellow flowers appear in great abundance during the Spring and again, but less generously in September. Very appreciated due to its spectacular, luminous flowers and its great vigour.

Its drought resistance and tolerance of poor, sandy oils and even rock crevices make it suitable for decorating rocky gardens, mixed with *Aubrieta, Campanula, Arabis, Armeria,Dianthus*, etc. Useful for filling in small spaces exposed to full sun. Has given rise to many cultivated varieties.

Must pruned after the spring flowering to keep it compact. Can be propagated by cuttings in June. Suitable for potting.

SP. Canastillo, Cestillo de oro, Alisón FR. Corbeille d'or GER. Steinkraut IT. Alisso.

9. *APTENIA CORDIFOLIA*
(*Mesembryanthemum cordifolium, Lithocarpus cordifolius*)

S.Africa - R - [PERENNE] - VI/IX - [PLENO SOL] - (-5°C) - [SOPORTA LA PROXIMIDAD DEL MAR] [MELIFERA] [TOLERA LA CONTAMINACIÓN DEL AIRE]

Baby sun rose

Graceful, carpeting succulent with creeping shoots and pleasant, tender, green, heart-shaped leaves. The tiny (1cm), purple flowers open in sunshine and the whole plant is a lover of hot, dry conditions.

The «red apple» variety (in the photograph), with its large (2cm), red flowers is very popular along with *Aptenia cordifolia* var. *variegata* which has leaves with white borders.

Best results (both for colour and flowering capacity) are obtained in full sun although it will also thrive in semi-shade. Ideal for covering both large and small, low maintenance surfaces. The most appropriate plant for greening up slopes and sunny rock gardens, or for hanging over walls.

Totally undemanding and easy to propagate from cuttings. Suitable for potting.

Curiously, it can be eaten as a vegetable, with a flavour not unlike spinach.

SP. Rocío FR. Ficoïde à feuilles de coeur   GER. - IT.: *Aptenia cordifolia.*

10.   *ARABIS CAUCASICA (Arabis albida)*

SE.Europe - M - [PERENNE] - III/IV - [FLOR PERFUMADA] [PLENO SOL] [MELIFERA]

Wall rock cress

Vigorous creeper with greyish leaves that reaches a height of 15cm. The white, lightly scented flowers normally appear in March or April but after mild winters as early as January or February. Often confused with the very similar *Arabis alpina*.

Good cover for small surfaces and rock gardens. Can be combined with *Aubrieta, Armeria, Alyssum,*etc to give pretty evergreen borders. Prefers non-chalky soils but will tolerate even poor substrates. Resistant to drought.

Amongst its cultivers, "Nana", of reduced size and "Snowflake" with larger flowers stand out.

Has a tendency to spread out so pruning after flowering is recommended. Seeds are sown in April and cuttings taken in May.

SP. *Arabis caucasica* FR. Corbeille d'argent, Arabette GER. Gebirgsgänsekresse
IT. Arabetta

11. *ARCTOSTAPHYLOS UVA-URSI*

Europe - L -  - IV/V -

Bearberry, Kinnikinnick, Trailing manzanita

Low, flat bush of creeping stems with adventitious roots which grows to 30cm. in height and to a diameter of 4m. The bright, rounded, leathery leaves redden in winter while the bell-shaped, pinkish-white flowers appear in Spring. Fruits are bright red with edible but sour pink, floury flesh. Makes a good mountain-garden plant as it requires a cold Winter with minimum temperatures around -7C. Will grow at low altitudes at a shady, north facing site. Resistant to drought and acidity although it prefers permeable, calcareous soils.

An excellent, highly ornamental cover plant, useful for containing unstable soils, slopes and hillsides. Very appropriate for rock-gardens. Can be propagated from lateral cuttings, in July, or by air layering with branches cut after two years growth.

A stimulating infusion of the leaves has medicinal properties.

SP. Gayuba, Uva de oso, Manzanilla de pastor, Manzanita   FR. Busserole, Raisin d'ours, Arbusier traînant GER. Bärentraube IT. Orsella, Uva ursina.

11

12.   *ARCTOTIS x HYBRIDUS*

S.Africa - M - ![PERENNE] - V/IX - ![PLENO SOL] - (-8°C.) - ![SOPORTA LA PROXIMIDAD DEL MAR]

African daisy

   Horticultural hybrid of the African species *A. Acaulis* and *A. breviscapa.* Pretty and vigorous plant with ranging stems and short silver-grey leaves. The glowing flowers, like large (7cm.) daisies come in bright yellows, oranges and reds throughout the Summer. They remain closed on overcast days, only opening in the sun. Requires dry, well drained soils that can be slightly alkaline.

   The «Orange» variety in the photograph is both vigorous and free flowering, reaching a height of 30cm. Forms good cover for small and medium areas in dry or rock gardens and on slopes. Mass plantations act as fire breaks. Suitable for potting and for cut flowers.

   Humidity must be avoided in the Winter and cuttings from young shoots, a favourite of snails, can be taken in April.

SP. Margarita africana,   FR.-GER.- IT.: *Arctotis X hybridus.*

13. *ARMERIA MARITIMA (Armeria vulgaris, Statice armeria)*

Europe - M -  - V/VIII - [☼ PLENO SOL] [SOPORTA LA PROXIMIDAD DEL MAR]

Trift

Small, grasslike cushion of grey-green leaves up to 20cm. tall. Very attractive with tall, pink-purple flowerheads. Very vigorous and resistant to drought and coastal conditions, tolerates poor, and soils.

Useful for carpeting small areas, spaces between rocks, dry corners, and for combining with other carpeting plants. Several cultivars exist. Among them: «Alba», with pretty white flowers, and «Vindictive», with bright pink flowers.

Withered inflorescences must be removed. Propagated via cuttings in Summer or by division in March/April.

SP. Césped de España, Césped del Olimpo, Césped marino FR. Oeillet de mer,
Gazon d 'Espagne GER. Strandgrasnelke IT. *Armeria maritima.*

14. *ARTEMISIA ARBORESCENS*

Mediterranean basin - M - - VI/VII - - (-8°C.) -

Wormwood

Feathery aromatic shrub around 1m. tall with superb, silky silver foliage. The leaves are incised, as if to filter the light. The small (1cm.), round, yellow flowers are hardly spectacular but the impressive structure of the leaves more than compensates for this. Recommended for all Mediterranean gardens. Thrives even in calcareous soils. Drought resistant but benefits from occasional watering.

Contrasts magnificently with red foliage or fruits (*Berberis, Cotoneaster*) and harmonizes with blue flowers. Wormwood shrubs are highly ornamental, cover the ground and act as fire breaks. Propagation is by terminal cuttings in September.

SP. Ajenjo, Ajenjo moruno FR. Armoise GER. Beifuss IT. Assenzio arboreo.

15. *ARTEMISIA* x 'POWIS CASTLE'

Horticultural-R -  - VI/VII -

Wormwood

Probably a hybrid between *A. absinthium* and *A. arborescens*. Lovely, rounded, dense bush some 60cm. tall and 120cm. wide with magnificent, aromatic foliage, slightly irregular and of a pretty silver grey colour.Planted in groups, a regular, flat-topped mass is formed. The flowers are of little ornamental value. Resistant to drought and poor stony soils but requires good drainage.

Excellent cover plant, in both small groups and large masses of great beauty. Prevents the advance of fire. Planting density of 2/m2. Removal of the dead flowers benefits the foliage and an annual pruning is required to prevent the base from becoming threadbare. Terminal cuttings can be taken in September.

SP. Artemisa plateada FR. Armoise GER. Beifuss IT. Assenzio.

16.   *ASPIDISTRA ELATIOR* (*Aspidistra lurida*)

China - L - [PERENNE] - VIII - [TOLERA LA SOMBRA] [SOMBRA] [TOLERA LA CAL] - (-3°C.) - [TOLERA LA CONTAMINACIÓN DEL AIRE] ✓

Cast iron plant, Parlour plant

A very popular pot plant that is seldom seen in gardens where it can be used very successfully as a cover plant in the darkest of corners. A robust rhizomatose shrub, with succulent roots that accept all, even calcareous soils. The large, very ornamental leaves, some 60-90cm. long are a dark, shiny green. The «Variegata» form has white leaf borders and is very attractive although it requires more light.

The small (2cm.) ,fleshy, stemless, solitary, opaque purple bell-shaped flowers appear during the Summer almost at ground level hidden amongst the leaves and are followed by globular fruits.

Cannot withstand direct sun but thrives under trees and in dense shade. A good backround plant for *Chlorophytum* and *Ajuga*. Can live for as long as a century. Benefits from a certain amount of humus and humidity in the soil. Excessively dry conditions open the way for red spider and cochineal attack. Propagation by rhizome division in March-April.

SP. Planta de hojas, Planta de portera, Hojas de salón   GER. Schieldnarbe, Sternschild, Schusterpalme   FR.-IT.: *Aspidistra elatior*

17. *ASTERISCUS MARITIMUS* (*Odontospermum maritimum*)

Mediterranean - M -  - IV/X - - (-5°C.) -

Gold coin

An extensive, dense bush some 15-20cm. high, with dark, grey-green leaves. Flowers plentifully over a long period with the bright yellow flowers positioned at the top of the plant.

Requires well drained, acid or neutral soils and is resistant to drought and coastal conditions. An excellent cover plant for small spaces and rocky gardens. Combines marvellously with *Rosmarinus*.

Can be sown in April with cuttings from young shoots best taken in August.

SP. Churrera, Estrellada de mar   FR. - GER.- IT.: *Asteriscus maritimus*

18. *ATRIPLEX HALIMUS*

Mediterranean - R - - VI/VIII -

Saltbrush

Small, squat bush with silver grey undulated leaves and branches up to 1.5m. high. The tiny, reddish grey flowers are of no ornamental value. Along with tolerance to drought its resistance to salt spray and salty soils make it ideal for coastal gardens.

An excellent covering mass for small and medium areas that, as well as providing an attractive backdrop for other plants, acts as a fire break. Must be pruned after flowering to keep it compact. Planting density: 1/m2, easily propagated via cuttings.

The leaves can be eaten as a salad or pickle. Sometimes cultivated as forage and frequently grown as a low hedge.

SP. Salado blanco, Salobre, Marisma, Orzaga FR. Pourpier de mer, Blanquette, Arroche GER. Melde IT. Porcellana marina, Alimo, Malocchia.

19.   *AUBRIETA DELTOIDEA* (*Aubrietia deltoidea*)

Italy - R - ![perenne] - IV/V - ![pleno sol] ![tollera la cal]

Purple rock-cress

Dense, creeping plant some 15-20cm. high with grey leaves and abundant purple flowers. Numerous varieties with blue, pink, lilac or red flowers exist. Prefers calcareous ground but will grow in any permeable soil.Drought resistant tolerant of partial shade although it flowers less. Shortlived.

Very pretty covering the ground close to Spring bulbs (*Narcissus*) or combined with other carpeting plants (*Armeria, Alyssum, Dianthus, Iberis*). Marvellous hanging from a wall.

Pruning to the ground after flowering prevents fruiting and stimulates growth. Sowing in March, cuttings in June and division in September.

SP. Aubretia FR. Aubriète GER. Blaukissen IT. Aubrezia.

20. *BACOPA CORDATA (Sutera cordata)*

C.America - R - 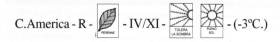 - IV/XI - - (-3°C.)

Ground-cover Sutera

Very dense carpeting mat with small indented, heart shaped leaves and numerous tiny white flowers appear almost at leaf-level from Spring through Autumn.

Grows in any soil and requires light, continuous humidity throughout the flowering period. Suitable for potting. Appreciates light shade and will stop flowering in direct Summer sun due to the excessive heat.

«Snowflake» in the photograph is an excellent cultivar while others with mauve and light pink flowers also exist. Propagation by seed or division in April.

SP: Nevada   FR. - GER. - IT.: *Bacopa cordata.*

21. *BELOPERONE GUTTATA* (*Justicia brandegeana*)

Mexico - R - [PERENNE] - V/XII - [TOLERA LA SOMBRA] [TOLERA LA CAL] - (0°C).

Shrimp plant, Prawn plant

Curious, ornamental cover plant for warm, frost free gardens. A shrub of arched, herbaceous stems growing to between 90 and 150cm. tall and wide. Easily identified due to the numerous attractive hanging inflorescences reminiscent of lobster tails.These are spikes some 10 to 20cm. long composed of red brown (or orange or pinkish depending on the observer) bracts and small white flowers which may adorn the plant throughout the year. The young leaves are an apple green colour.

Accepts both acid and calcareous soils as long as they are light and organic. Requires frequent Summer watering. Suitable for covering the ground in half-shaded flowerbeds and rock gardens. Good in pots and containers.»Yellow Queen» is a variety with yellow-green bracts.

Benefits from a stong annual pruning to keep it low and compact. Softwood cuttings, if possible from flowerless branches and treated with rooting powder are taken in June.

SP. Camarón, Corazón, Lúpulo de interior FR. Plante crevette,

GER. - IT.: *Beloperone guttata.*

22. *BERGENIA CRASSIFOLIA*
(Bergenia bifolia, Saxifraga crassifolia)

Siberia - L - 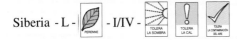 - I/IV -

Siberian tea

Strikingly shaped plant, highly thought of for of its pretty foliage and lovely, abundant, early flowers. Presents large, fleshy, shiny, spoon-shaped leaves that become mahogany-coloured in the cold. The rhizomes spread slowly to form a mat that covers the ground. Attractive pinky-blue flowers appear in the Winter. Drought resistant and will grow in all, even calcareous, soils.

Good cover for small or medium areas, under trees or in shade. Withstands deep shade and even direct sun as long as the ground is cool. Can be grown with spring bulbs (*Narcissus*), blue violets, or combined with shade-loving carpeting plants (*Helxine,Saxifraga sarmentosa, Viola hederacea, Ajuga*, etc.). Best planted at a density of 5m2. Division in Spring, after flowering, or in Autumn. A healthy, disease-free plant, the leaves of which can be used to make a stimulant infusion. Suitable for potting, the flowers are useful for making bouquets.

SP. Hortensia de invierno GER. Steinbrech FR.- IT.: *Bergenia crassifolia.*

23.　*BIDENS FERULIFOLIA*

S.Arizona - R - ![PERENNE] - IV-XI - ![FLOR PERFUMADA] ![PLENO SOL] - (-5°C.)

Fern leaved beggar-ticks

A lively, short-lived, creeping plant, much appreciated for its extremely abundant flowers. The leaves are fine and divided into filiform segments while the yellow starlike flowers resemble small, simple dahlias and produce a light honey-like scent that attracts bees and butterflies.Fast growing,(up to 50cm.), in any soil and full sun but best kept short through light pruning. Several more compact varieties exist.

Ideal, free flowering ground cover plant, suitable for rocky areas, it mixes to wonderful effect with *Verbena, Agathaea, Felicia,* and *Scáevola*. Suitable for potting. Will flower throughout the whole year if the Winter is mild and frost free. Propagated by cuttings in Spring or Autumn.

SP. Verbena amarilla　　　　　　　　　　　　FR. - GER. - IT.:　*Bidens ferulifolia.*

24. *BILLBERGIA NUTANS*

Brazil - L -  PERENNE -II/IV - TOLERA LA SOMBRA - (-2°C.)

Queen's tears

The silver-lined, olive green leaves of this terrestrial bromeliad form dense groups that redden in the sun. Reaches heights of 45cm. The attractive flowers with yellow-green petals bordered in blue and reddish sepals, emerge as hanging racemes from the pink bracts towards the end of the Winter.

Adaptable but prefers slightly acidic, fibrous soil. Withstands short, light frosting. Can store rain or irrigation water to create the required conditions due to its funnel-like shape. Forms good cover for small areas when planted en masse in semi-shade under trees. The numerous plantlets that develop can be separated from the base of the adult plant in May. A highly sought-after hybrid *Billbergia x Windii*, similar but with wider leaves and bigger flowers, has been developed.

SP. Lágrimas de la reina, Avena de salón FR. Pleurs de la reine GER. Zimmerhafer IT. *Billbergia nutans.*

25. *BRACHYCOME MULTIFIDA (Brachyscome multifida)*

E.Australia - R - [PERENNE] - III/X - [PLENO SOL] - (-7°C.)

Cutleaf daisy, Rock daisy

Bright, graceful, toloniferous, creeping shrublet, with finely divided leaves that grows vigorously up to 15-20cm. tall. The blue or mauve, daisy-like flowers are produced profusely over a long period. Fairly resistant to drought.

Long lasting masses of flowers form excellent cover for sunny slopes and rocky areas. Combines well with *Diascia* and *Bidens*. Good pot plant.

Seeds best sown in April, with plant division in Autumn and Spring.

SP. Vitadinia azul   FR. -GER.- IT.: *Brachycome multifida.*

26. *BUPLEURUM FRUTICOSUM*

S.Europe - M -  - IV/VIII - PLENO SOL — TOLERA LA SOMBRA — SOPORTA LA PROXIMIDAD DEL MAR — MELIFERA — TOLERA LA CONTAMINACIÓN DEL AIRE

Hare's ear

Low, round, graceful, many branched and aromatic shrub with leathery, oblong, shiny leaves that give off a strong resinous scent when rubbed. Seagreen leaves and umbels of golden-green flowers. Reaches a height of 1.5-2m. Vigorous and highly resistant to drought, accepting dry, arid soils, well drained and preferably acidic. At home in half shade under pine trees.

Excellent cover plant for Mediterranean flower beds when planted at a density of 2m2. Pretty combined with *Teucrium fruticans,* also used for loose hedges. Pruned lightly in March-April. Propagated via half-woody cuttings or seed in September. Medicinal (fruits and roots used as a cough remedy). An extract of the roots is used for fishing in Corsica.

SP. Adelfilla, Matabuey FR. Buplèvre ligneux, Oreille de lièvre GER. Hasenohr
IT. *Bupleurum fruticosum.*

27.   *CALLISTEMON VIMINALIS* 'Little John'

SE.Australia - M - PERENNE - IV/VII - PLENO SOL - (-5°C.) - SOPORTA LA PROXIMIDAD DEL MAR   MELIFERA

Bottle Brush

   Miniature horticultural variety some 50 to 90cm. high with pretty, grey foliage. Silky young leaves are pinkish-bronze.   The garnet coloured flowers, brush-shaped with long stamens, appear intermittently throughout the year, especially between April and June or after a storm. Drought tolerant although occasional watering is beneficial. Prefers a sunny position with light, organic and slightly calcareous soil.

   Good cover for rockeries, flowerbeds and slopes. Combines well with groups of *Artemisia, Ceanothus, Cistus, Lavandula, Rosmarinus* and *Westringia.* Suitable for containers.

   May benefit from pruning after flowering. Propagation is by half-woody cuttings in July. The nectar laden flowers attract certain birds.

SP. Limpiatubos enano, Escobilla enana FR. Rince-bouteille GER. *Callistemon*

IT. Scovolino da bottiglie.

28. CALLUNA VULGARIS (Erica vulgaris)

Europe - M -  - IX/XI -

Heather, Scotch heather

Attractively shaped bush up to 1m. tall with contorted branches and erect shoots, fine foliage and delicate, pinky-purple flowers. Withstands poor, dry soils but not alkalinity. Will not tolerate excess humidity.

Good cover for both small and large areas, even in semi-shade under trees. Combines well with *Aucuba, Fatsia* and *Skimmia*. Several cultivated varieties exist.

Requires pruning after flowering to maintain density. Does not succumb to plagues or disease. Can be propagated from cuttings treated with rooting powder in August.

SP. Brecina FR. Bruyère commune GER. Besenheide IT. Brugo

29.   *CAMPANULA MURALIS (Campanula portenschlagiana)*

Dalmatia - L - - V/VII -

Dalmatian bellflower

A very widespread plant, very beautiful and interesting, which grows, grasslike, into dense mats some 15cm. thick with shiny, rounded leaves of a pretty green colour and abundant, lilac-blue, bell-shaped flowers 2cm. across. Flowering occurs throughout the Spring and Summer and again in September. Although a plant of semi-shade it will tolerate both direct sun and full shade.

Very useful for greening up small areas in partial shade. Admirably suited to the decoration of walls, pavings and shaded rockeries where attractive flower carpets are formed. Very beautiful alongside stone, or (in the sun) the yellow flowers of *Senecio saxifraga*. Suitable for potting.

Easily propagated by division of mats in the Autumn. Beware! Highly thought of by slugs.

SP. Campanilla dálmata Fr. Campanule dalmatienne GER. Dalmatiner glockenblume IT. *Campanula muralis*.

30. *CARPOBROTUS EDULIS (Mesembryanthemum edule)*

S.Africa - R -  - III/IV - - (-6°C.) -

Hottentot fig

Vigorous, creeping succulent plant reaching lengths of several metres, with thick leaves the size of the index finger and in Spring, large (10cm. diameter) yellow or purple flowers. Forms dense carpets some 15cm. thick, that should not be trodden on, potentially over large areas. Tolerates salty soil and is highly resistant to drought. Used to colonise dry, coastal slopes and bluffs, to coat high walls and to stabilise sandy dunes. Cuttings taken in Spring or Autumn can be planted 'in situ' at a density of 5m2. Suitable for pots.

The figlike fruit are edible and the fleshy leaves can be consumed as a vegetable.

SP. Bálsamo, Uña de león, Higo marino FR. Figuier des hottentots, Griffe de sourcière GER. Pferdefeige IT. Fico degli ottentotti.

31.　*CASSIA CORYMBOSA (Senna corymbosa)*

Argentina - R - ![SEMPERENNE] - VIII/XI - ![PLENO SOL] ![TOLERA LA CAL] - (-9°C.) - ![SOPORTA LA PROXIMIDAD DEL MAR]

Flowering senna, Scrambled eggs

The flowers of this vigorous, rounded shrub make it highly decorative. The arched branches carry light green leaves and, at the end of the Summer, clusters of golden-yellow flowers. Accepts all, even basic soils and is drought resistant.

Covers the soil, alone or in groups. «A. Boehm» is an excellent variety for cultivation in containers. To maintain a low, covering shrub a prune to 30-40cm. is needed in March or April. Propagation by seed in Spring or by mature cuttings in July-August.

SP. Casia de Buenos Aires FR. Séné GER. Kassie IT. *Cassia.*

32. *CEANOTHUS THYRSIFLORUS* VAR. *REPENS*

California - M - - III/VI -

Creeping blue blossom

An attractive, creeping bush, both dense and vigorous. Perfect ground cover, some 40cm. high and 1.5m. across. Rounded bunches of delicate blue flowers appear amongst the shiny green foliage in Spring and often again in Autumn. Although tolerant of alkalinity a slightly acidic, sandy soil is prefered. Will not accept clay. Drought resistant and tolerant of partial shade.

Unbeatable cover for arid rockeries and slopes when planted at a density of 1-2/m2. Suitable for containers.

Benefits from light pruning after the Spring flowering. Tender cuttings in April, woody in October. May suffer from chlorosis due to iron deficiency in basic soils.

SP. Ceanoto, Lila de California FR. Céanothe GER. Säckelblume IT. Ceanoto.

33.   *CENTAUREA CANDIDISSIMA*   *(Centaurea rutifolia* **var.** *candidissima, Centaurea cineraria, Senecio candidissima)*

Sicily - M - ![PERENNE] - VII/VIII - ![PLENO SOL] ![TOLERA LA CAL] ![SOPORTA LA PROXIMIDAD DEL MAR]

Dusty miller

A wide, elegant plant, dense and extensively branched with pale, silver-grey, velvety, pinnate leaves some 20cm. long.

Golden-yellow inflorescences large and showy. «Argentea» variety has incised leaves.

Very resistant to drought and inhospitable terrain: tolerates both lime and the proximity of the sea. Good as cover in dry gardens (slopes, rockeries, flowerbeds) where it contrasts strikingly with other flowers and foliage.

Old, withered flowers should be removed. Sowing and division in October or March.

SP. Blanquilla FR. Centaurée cinéraire   GER. - IT.: *Centaurea candidissima.*

34. *CENTAUREA PULCHERRIMA (Aeteopappus pulcherrimus)*

Caucasus - R -  - V/VII - [PLENO SOL] [TOLERA LA CAL] - (-5°C.) - [SOPORTA LA PROXIMIDAD DEL MAR]

Star-thistle

Pretty, compact mass of highly incised, magnificent silver-grey leaves, up to 80cm. high. Bright pink flowerlets collected into solitary, star-shaped heads. Often confused with the similar, yellow-flowered *Centaurea ragusina*.

Resists drought and thrives in any well drained soil, even calcareous. Excellent ornamental species, especially if planted in clumps alternating with reds and blues. Suitable for containers. Highly recommended.

Sown in March, cuttings in July.

SP. Centaurea FR. Centaurée GER. Kornblume IT. Centaurea.

35. *CENTRADENIA ROSEA*
(Centradenia inaequilateralis, Heterocentron roseum)

Mexico - R - [SEMPERENNE] - X/V - [PLENO SOL] [TOLERA LA SOMBRA] - (-2°C.)

Pearl flower

Small creeping mat with elliptical, paired leaves some 3-5cm. long, ciliated, rough to the touch with red undersides. Stems are quadrangular, reddish and also ciliated. Numerous showy flowers with four, bright red-purple petals and stamens of unequal length. Grows up to between 30 and 60cm.

Highly decorative, easily cultivated plant which thrives in any, preferably fresh and organic soil. October to May flowering period generally interrupted by a short Winter break. There is also a Summer resting period. Resists temperatures below –2°C. (down to around –5°C.), losing all foliage in Winter. Growth begins again in the Spring. Cuttings in April.

SP. Perla de Cuba

FR.- GER.- IT.: *Centradenia rosea.*

36. *CENTRANTHUS RUBER (Kentranthus ruber)*

S.Europe - M - [PERENNE] - V/IX - [FLOR PERFUMADA] [PLENO SOL] [TOLERA LA SOMBRA] [TOLERA LA CAL] [TOLERA LA CONTAMINACIÓN DEL AIRE]

Red valerian

Vigorous, fast growing shrub with erect stems up to 60cm. tall. Sea-green leaves and perfumed groups of red flowerlets. «Albus» produces white flowers. Coloniser of ruins which often becomes naturalised around gardens. An excellent plant for inhospitable gardens as it will tolerate the poorest soils and longest droughts.

Planted at 3/m2 but will reseed easily. Useful for giving colour to rockeries, walls and crags and for flowerbed composition along with *Thymus, Lavandula, Salvia officinalis, Teucrium, Rosamarinus, Westringia,* etc. Used to recolonise degraded areas. Suitable for pots and cut flowers. Prune after flowering has finished. Propagated easily by seed.

Medicinal, with anti-convulsive properties.

SP. Veleriana roja, Milamores, Disparates FR. Valériane rouge GER. Spornblume

IT. Centranto.

37. CERASTIUM TOMENTOSUM

Italy - R -  - IV/VI -

Chickweed

Classic, aggresive cover plant, appreciated for its colour, adaptability and abundant, delicate white flowers popular with butterflies. Dense, silver-grey foliage. A sunshine plant, vigorous and frugal in all climates and substrates. Withstands drought but needs occasional watering if it is to keep its leaves throughout the Summer. Planted at a density of 4/m2.

Can replace grass on dry soils. Forms an excellent colour contrasting carpet some 15cm. high for slopes and rocky gardens. Good for both large and small areas: acts as a fire break. Needs regular pruning to prevent thinning out.

Propagation simple: either by direct seeding or bundles of cuttings on the soil in October or March.

SP. Cerastio FR. Céraiste GER. Hornkraut IT. Cerastio

38. *CERATOSTIGMA GRIFFITHII*

Himalayas - R -  - IX/X -

Burmese Plumbago

Interesting creeping mat, compact and extensively branched, growing up to 80cm. high. Pleasant, delicate-green foliage turns scarlet in Autumn when pretty, bright blue flowers appear.

Withstands a certain amount of drought but appreciates occasional watering. Light cosmetic pruning in March is beneficial. No known diseases or plagues. Propagated from lateral shoot cuttings in July.

SP. Galaxia   FR. - GER. - IT.: *Ceratostigma griffithii*

39. *CERATOSTIGMA PLUMBAGINOIDES*
(Plumbago larpentae)

China - M -  - VIII/X -

Dwarf Plumbago, Blue leadwort

Vigorous, spreading, deciduous creeper only 15cm. high. Highly thought of cover due to the attractive bronze hues of the Autumn foliage and the remarkable, long-lasting, midnight-blue flowers. Rustic and adaptable to poor, arid, even calcareous soils. Periodic Summer watering is appreciated. May become invasive and displace weaker species over time.

Used to carpet large and small areas, at a density of 5/m2. Avoid excess damp and prune to the ground in March. Division in March, or softwood cuttings in May.
SP. - FR. - GER. - IT.: *Plumbago.*

!

40. *CHLOROPHYTUM COMOSUM*
(Chlorophytum elatum, Chlorophytum capense)

S.Africa - R -  - VI/VII -

Spider plant

A very popular pot plant, interesting as a ground cover for shady areas in mild climates. It has fleshy roots and a central crown of elegant, curved leaves from which the long flowering stems arise. The flowers are insignificant but give rise by vivipary to new rosettes which curve down to the ground. These root easily around the parent producing good ground cover which can support full shade.

The form «Vittatum» (in the photo) has green leaves with a central white stripe. «Variegatum» is more vigorous with longer leaves with white margins.

If placed high this is an attractive hanging plant. It will survive in any soil including calcareous but requires a degree of humidity. It is easy to propagate by separation of new rosettes in Spring or Autumn.

SP. Cintas, Mala madre   GER. Liliengrün   FR.- IT. *Chlorophytum.*

41. *CHRYSANTHEMUM FRUTESCENS*
(Anthemis frutescens, Argyranthemum frutescens)

Canary Islands - R -  - IV/VI - ☀ - (-4°C.) -

White marguerite, Paris daisy

A low, round, compact shrub up to 1 m. in height, with divided leaves. The white flowers are abundant in Spring with, usually, a second flowering in Autumn. In mild climates it can flower throughout the year. It prospers in almost all soil types and has many cultivars with yellow, pink and blue flowers and with double-flowered forms. It is a good ground cover but requires regular watering. Pruning the dead flowers prolongs the flowering period. It is easily propagated by cuttings taken from young shoots in March-April or in September.

SP. Margarita, Margarita de bola   FR. Marguerite   GER. Strauchmargerite

IT. Margherita.

42. *CINERARIA MARITIMA*

(Senecio cineraria, Senecio maritima)

Mediterranean - R - - VI/IX -

Silver groundsel

Shrub up to 1m. tall. Wide and loose, cultivated for the beauty of its leaves. These are deeply incised and covered with a silvery-white fluff. In the Summer the unremarkable yellow flowers are best removed as soon as possible to benefit the foliage (which has a tendancy to become spindly). Extremely vigorous, happy in even basic soils and tolerant of both drought and the proximity of the sea. Incombustible, can prevent the spread of fire if planted en masse. Beautiful cultivars such as «Candicans», «Diamond» and «Silver Dust» exist.

Very useful on slopes and rockeries or when planted as contrasting, ornamental, clumps. Propagated by cuttings taken before or after flowering.

SP. Cineraria, Rosa de mar FR. Cinéraire maritime GER. Cinerarie IT. Cineraria.

43.   *CISTUS ALBIDUS*

S. Europa - M - [PERENNE] - IV/V - [PLENO SOL] [TOLERA LA CAL] [SOPORTA LA PROXIMIDAD DEL MAR]

Rockrose

Robust, undemanding bush 1m. tall with pretty grey, velvety leaves and luminous pink spring flowers. Resistant to drought and poor, arid soils. Of the genus it is the species that best tolerates alkali soils. Hard to burn, can prevent fire if planted on a large scale. The «Albus» variety has white flowers.

Does not react well to transplanting: best sown directly into pots. Needs no more than a light prune of dry and damaged stems after flowering. Sowing in March, half woody cuttings in July and woody cuttings in May. Could be used as a support for truffle cultivation.

SP. Estepa blanca, Jara blanca FR. Ciste cotonneux GER. Zistrose IT. Cisto.

44. *CISTUS x PURPUREUS*

Mediterranean - M - - IV/V - -

Orchid rockrose

Woody, dense bush which grows up to 1.5m. high. Thin, lanceolate, somewhat undulate, dark green leaves. Large (7.5cm. across), violet-pink flowers with a dark purple patch at the base of each petal. Gives off a characteristic aroma during warm, dry weather. Drought resistant and tolerant of all soil types.

Interesting cover for dry gardens and sloping ground. Clumps in flower are a spectacular display. Hard to transplant: best obtained in pots. Pruning should be limited to a light trim and removal of dead and damaged limbs when flowering is complete. Cuttings from terminal buds in October. The leaves contain tannins, conferring resistance to fungal attack.

SP. Jara purpúrea FR. Ciste GER. Zistrose IT. Cisto.

45.   *CLIVIA MINIATA (Imantophyllum miniatum)*

S.Africa - L - PERENNE - II-IV - TOLERA LA SOMBRA TOLERA LA CAL - (-l°C.) - SOPORTA LA PROXIMIDAD DEL MAR TOLERA LA CONTAMINACIÓN DEL AIRE

Kafir lily

Considered an interior or patio plant which also thrives in mild, shady gardens. Tuberous roots and beautiful orange-red (brick-red) flowers emerging amongst a fan of leaves make the whole plant highly ornamental. All soils, even calcareous, are suitable provided there is enough organic matter present. Withstands Winter temperatures down to –7°C. but the leaves drop at –2 °C. only to reshoot in the Spring. Suitable for potting.

Covers the ground around shaded rocks and under trees if planted in groups. Suffers if watered excessively. Large slugs can decimate the foliage. Withered flowers best removed as the fruit, although decorative, weaken the plant. Flowers good in cut bunches. Division in Spring after flowering is complete.

SP. Clivia, Azucena cafre FR. Clivia GER. Riemenblatt IT. Clivia.

46. CONVALLARIA MAJALIS

Europe - R -  - IV/V - FLOR PERFUMADA | TOLERA LA SOMBRA | SOMBRA | SÓLO SUELO ÁCIDO

Lily of the valley

Graceful plant with surface creeping rhizomes and fresh foliage that drops in the Winter. The delicious white flowers with their wonderful perfume are suitable for small bouquets. The small, red fruits are also decorative.

A shade plant which prefers cool, acidic, humus rich soils but will tolerate any other type. A good cover plant for small and medium shaded areas such as copses. Suitable for potting. Avoid nitrogen fertilisers. Leaves can be cut with care at the end of Winter: the whole plant is highly toxic. Propagated by rhizome division after the Spring flowering period.

SP. Muguete, Lirio de los valles FR. Muguet de mai GER. Maiglöckchen
IT. Mughetto.

47. *CONVOLVULUS ARGENTEUS* *(Convolvulus cneorum)*

.Mediterranean - M - - IV/VI - - (-8°C.) -

Silverbush, Bush morning glory

Very ornamental carpeting plant some 50cm. high. Remarkable silky leaves with a silver sheen and pretty, bell-shaped flowers: white with pink streaks. Forms an extensive but compact, rounded, silvery mass. Flowers appear in Spring but may continue throughout the Summer.

Requires well drained, preferably calcareous soils that can be poor and arid. Recommended to embellish rockeries and slopes and planted as spectacular clumps which act as fire breaks. Good hanging from a wall or combined with *Teucrium fruticans*. Appreciates sporadic Summer watering. Best replaced after three years as the plants degrade with age. Seeding in March-April, cuttings from July to August.

SP. Campanilla plateada FR. Liseron GER. Winde IT. Convolvolo.

48. *CONVOLVULUS MAURITANICUS*
(Convolvulus mauritianus, Convolvulus sabatius)

N.Africa - R -  - IV/IX - ![PLENO SOL] ![TOLERA LA CAL] - (-7°C.) - ![SOPORTA LA PROXIMIDAD DEL MAR]

Ground morning-glory

Vigorous perennial with prostrate, herbaceous stems and few branches which forms a dense layer some 25cm. thick. Highly thought of for its long flowering period. The violet-blue flowers some 3-5cm. in diameter open only in the morning. Leaves rounded and blunt. Drought resistant and suitable for poor, arid, preferably calcareous soil. Apt for covering small spaces or as a hanging plant. Widely used on slopes and rockeries at a density of 3/m2. Beautiful combined with *Cerastium tomentosum*. Suitable for pots.

Periodic Summer watering extends the flowering period. Sowing in March-April, cuttings in March or September.

SP. Campanilla azul FR. Liseron GER. Winde IT. Convolvolo.

49.   COPROSMA REPENS (Coprosma baueri)

N.Zealand - R -   - (-5°C.) -

Mirror plant

Dioecious (unisexual individuals) shrub of great interest due to its foliage. Reaches heights of up to 6m. but can be kept much lower (70-120cm.) through pruning. Thick, oval leaves some 6-8cm. long shine brightly if grown in the sun. Small white flowers are of no ornamental value, but the yellow-orange female fruits are quite decorative.

Two interesting varieties have been developed: «Picturata» with mottled, pale yellow, almost white leaves and «Variegata» which, in the juvenile stage, has broad cream bands around the leaf edges. Both require full sun to maintain their colour. Partial to light, fresh, fertile soils but will tolerate even calcareous ground. Drought resistant and suitable for containers. Reacts well to pruning: useful for cover at any desired height. Good as a seaside hedge. Propagation by woody cuttings in March.

SP. Planta espejo   GER. Spiegelstrauch   FR.- IT.: *Coprosma repens*

49

50.　*CORONILLA GLAUCA (Coronilla valentina glauca)*

Mediterranean - R -  - II/IV - -

Crown vetch

Dense, light green bush up to 1m. high. Very useful to the gardener as it has abundant bright yellow, long-lasting flowers with a daytime perfume. Drought resistant and tolerant of all soils. Will grow in both damp conditions and in half shade. Reseeds spontaneously to the stage of choking gardens.

Good cover plant (planted at a density of 2/m2) whose bright flowers contrast beautifully with: *Viburnum tinus, Teucrium fruticans, Rosmarinus* and *Cotoneaster lactea.* «Citrina» is a surprising variety with wonderful, pale yellow flowers.

Does not tolerate harsh pruning: the limit being a light trim after flowering is comple-te. Sowing and cuttings at the end of Summer. Spring and Autumn seedlings can be taken from the garden. Suitable for containers

SP. Carolina FR.. Coronille GER. Kronwicke IT. Coronilla.

51. *COTONEASTER HORIZONTALIS*

W.China - M -  - IV/V - (icons: FLOR PERFUMADA, PLENO SOL, TOLERA LA SOMBRA, TOLERA LA CAL, SOPORTA LA PROXIMIDAD DEL MAR, MELIFERA, TOLERA LA CONTAMINACIÓN DEL AIRE)

Rock cotoneaster

Horizontal, deciduous shrub, branching out like a fish skeleton. Spacious and rigid, 0.5-1m. high with pretty, dark green, rounded leaves which take on attractive red hues come Autumn. Abundant, decorative, red fruit are a source of winter food for birds. Tolerant of poor, dry, arid and calcareous soils. Excellent seasonal cover, especially for rock gardens.

«Saxatilis» variety is smaller and fan shaped. «Variegatus» has leaves mottled with white, red in the Autumn.

Pruning in March. Grows well from seed, but the varieties must be grown from apical cuttings taken in July. Suitable for containers.

SP. - FR.- GER.- IT.: *Cotoneaster horizontalis.*

52.   COTONEASTER 'SKOGHOLM'
(Cotoneaster 'Skogsholmen', Cotoneaster dammeri 'Skogholm')

China - R -  - IV/V -

Bearberry cotoneaster

Spàcious bush with large arched branches which root on contact with the ground. Grows to 60cm. high and 3m. across at a rate of 1m./year. Leaves small, shiny and elliptical. Rare white flowers occasionally give rise to red fruits. Tolerant of both drought and poor soils.

Excellent cover for both large and small areas , for example under trees. Requires a light annual prune in April. Can be propagated from apical cuttings taken in September. Suitable for containers.

SP. -FR.- GER.- IT.: *Cotoneaster* 'skogholm'

53.   *CRASSULA MULTICAVA (Crassula punctata)*

S.Africa - R - [PERENNE] - IV - [PLENO SOL] [TOLERA LA SOMBRA] - (-3°C.) - [SOPORTA LA PROXIMIDAD DEL MAR] [TOLERA LA CONTAMINACIÓN DEL AIRE]

Crassula multicava

Succulent ground cover plant, named after the pits on the upper surface of its blue-green leaves. These take on a red tinge in the Summer sun. Delicate pink, almost white star-shaped Spring flowers grow on elongated stems and are followed by shoots and consequent branching. Grows up to 15cm. tall. Tolerant of any soil and by nature to drought. Will grow in shade but tends to lose colour and become spindly. Withered flowers should be removed.

Excellent cover for dry areas, both large and small. Easily reproduced from May cuttings. Suitable for potting.

SP. -FR.- GER.- IT.: *Crassula multicava.*

54.   *CUPHEA HYSSOPIFOLIA*

Guatemala - M -  PERENNE - IV/XI - PLENO SOL / TOLERA LA SOMBRA - (-2°C.) - MELIFERA

False heather

Graceful shrub, compact with many flexible branches 40-70cm. tall and small, shiny, dark green leaves. Tiny, delicate, pink or purple flowers appear in Spring through Autumn. «Alba», with white flowers is widely cultivated. Leaves drop at –3°C. but the plant survives down to –5°C. as a deciduous perennial. Thrives in all reasonably fertile soils but is susceptible to drought.

A prodigious flowerer, beautiful in clumps. Also an excellent pot and rock plant. Propagated from cuttings, tender in April or half-woody in October. Flowering branches are best removed after flowering is complete.

SP. Falsa brecina   FR. -GER.- IT.: *Cuphea hyssopifolia*

55.   *CUPHEA IGNEA   (Cuphea platycentra)*

Mexico - R -  - IV/XI - - (-1ºC.)

Cigar flower

Graceful shrub, spreading, with bright scarlet, black and white mouthed tubular flowers 2-3cm. long which resemble lit cigarettes. Long flowering period, even in the shade. Needs light, well drained organic soil. Useful as ground cover, planted en masse,(11/m2). «Variegata» has leaves marked with yellow, «Alba» has white flowers

Suitable for potting. Leaves drop at –2ºC. but the plant survives at –3ºC. Advisable to cut stems down to one third at the end of Winter. Ages rapidly, replacements required every 2-3 years. Propagated from lateral shoot cuttings in April.

SP. Cigarillo   FR. Fleur cigarette   GER. -IT. *Cuphea ignea*

56.   *CUPHEA MICROPETALA (Cuphea eminens)*

Mexico - R - - VII/XI -   - (-1°C.) -

Cuphea micropetala

Highly interesting and decorative perennial evergreen: up to 70cm. tall. The attractive, tubular flowers, 3-4cm. long, orange-yellow with green tips, appear in Summer and Autumn. Lanceolate leaves are 5-6cm. long. A temperate plant, drought resistant and at home in permeable soils, even if poor and calcareous.

Leaves deteriorate at –2°C. but survive down to –3°C., sprouting again in the Spring. Suitable for containers. An invigorating prune of two thirds of the lengths of the stems is advisable at the end of Winter. Useful forming striking clumps, especially alternated with *Rosmarinus, Felicia amoena, Hebe, Nepeta, Salvia, Scaevola*, etc. Propagation from tender cuttings in April.

SP. Cúfea   FR. -GER. -IT.: *Cuphea micropetala*

57.   *CYMBALARIA MURALIS (Linaria cymbalaria)*

Europe - R - [PERENNE] - IV/IX - [SOMBRA] [TOLERA LA SOMBRA] [TOLERA LA CAL] [TOLERA LA CONTAMINACIÓN DEL AIRE]

Kenilworth ivy

Pretty, herbaceous creeper with long hanging or trailing stems that forms a carpet some 15cm. thick. The small, tender green leaves, similar to those of ivy contrast pleasantly during the Spring and Summer with yellow throated, pale lilac-blue flowers. Drought resistant if planted in the shade. Will naturalise easily in favourable conditions. Varieties with white flowers and variegated leaves have been developed.

Perfect for north facing walls and rockeries, gaps between pavings and small shaded areas. Propagated easily from seed in March-April or by cuttings from stems with adventitious roots, in April.

SP. Picardía, Juntapulpa, Palomilla de muro FR. Linaire, Ruines de Rome

GER. Leinkraut IT. Edera fiorita.

58. *CYRTOMIUM FALCATUM (Polystichum falcatum)*

E.Asia - M - [PERENNE] [TOLERA LA SOMBRA] [SOMBRA] - (-7°C.) - [TOLERA LA CONTAMINACIÓN DEL AIRE]

Holly fern

Robust and attractive rhizomatose fern, whose strange similarity to palm trees makes it highly ornamental. Forms a broad shrub, 50 to 90cm. high, with shiny, rigid fronds and leaflets reminiscent of holly leaves. Tolerant to short periods of drought but requires a shaded site. Grows in any soil but the optimum is cool and rich in humus.

Interesting cover for shaded areas and under trees. Very pretty next to stone or wood. Suitable for potting. "Rochfordianum (or Rochefordii)" is a smaller variety,40 to 50cm. tall, less resistant to the cold, with wider fronds and short, thick, indented leaflets.

Remove the withered fronds regularly. Propagation by division in the Spring.

SP. -FR.- GER.- IT.: *Cyrtomium.*

59.   DIANTHUS CAESIUS (Dianthus gratianopolitanus)

Europe - M - ![PERENNE] - V/VII - ![FLOR PERFUMADA] ![PLENO SOL] ![TOLERA LA CAL] ![SOPORTA LA PROXIMIDAD DEL MAR] ![TOLERA LA CONTAMINACIÓN DEL AIRE]

Cheddar pink, Garden pink

This miniature pink forms an extensive cushion of bluish, almost silver leaves crowned between May and July with simple but highly perfumed, pink flowers. Drought resistant but benefits from occasional Summer watering. Thrives in poor, arid soil, preferably sandy and calcareous and only in full sun.Short lived but reseeds spontaneously in most gardens. Varieties with white, red, various shades of pink and double flowers exist.The photo shows the cultivar «Badenia».

A highly thought of carpeting plant for small foreground areas, wall crevices, rockeries, etc. Combines well with *Arabis, Armeria, Aubrieta* and *Alyssum*. Suitable for potting.

Requires liming in acid soils. Easily propagated from June cuttings, or by Spring or Autumn division. Popular with butterflies.

SP. Clavellina rocosa, Clavellina cespitosa FR. Oeillet bleuatre GER. Pfingstnelke IT. Garofano.

60. *DIANTHUS PLUMARIUS*
(Dianthus moschatus, Dianthus arenarius)

S.Europe - R -  - V/IX -

Cottage pink

Robust, very vigorous species, forming wide mats of fine, sea-green leaves. Abundant, single or double flowers are exquisitely perfumed. Most are pink or white with a wavy fringe. Many varieties exist, such as «White reserve» in the photo, a profuse flowerer.

This ancient, wild pink, sometimes hard to find, forms excellent cover in full sun or light shade. Very popular, due to its prolonged flowering period, as decoration for rockeries, low walls and small areas of light, well-drained soil. Suitable for potting. Reaches heights of 30cm. when in flower.

Liming needed in acidic soils. Propagation via June cuttings or by Spring or Autumn division. Much frequented by butterflies.

SP. Clavel coronado Fr. Oeillet mignardise GER. Federnelke IT. Garafano piumoso.

61. *DIASCIA BARBERAE*

S.Africa - R - [PERENNE] - V/X - [PLENO SOL] [TOLERA LA SOMBRA] - (-5°C.)

Twinspur

Graceful creeping perennial, some 30cm. tall, carpeting the ground with small, shiny leaves and attractive, long lasting flowers that are pink, 2cm. across with two spurs. Leaves dark green, oval and somewhat toothed.

Thrives in light, fresh, nutrient rich soils. Very useful for the colour of its flowers which combines strikingly with *Bidens, Brachcome* and *Campanula*. Suitable for potting. Useful for carpeting small areas and rockeries. «Ruby field» (a hybrid between *Diascia cordata* and *D. barberae*) has heart-shaped leaves and survives down to -9 °C.

Removal of withered blooms prolongs the flowering period until October-November. Pruning to within 5cm. of the ground in April promotes beneficial branching. Sowing and separation of rooted fragments in April.

SP. Rosada   FR. -GER. -IT. : *Diascia*

62. *DICHONDRA REPENS (Dichondra micrantha)*

Tropics - R - ⬚ - ⬚ ⬚ - (-9°C.) - ⬚ ⬚

Lawn-leaf, Wonder leaf

Stoloniferous carpeting plant, caespitose and highly interesting, with small, rounded, fresh-green leaves, 1-2cm. long which appear to be dense, forming excellent ground cover resistant to light trampling. A good alternative to traditional grass lawns with the advantage of not requiring regular mowing. Reaches heights of 2-3cm. in full sun but in the shade, or with regular watering grows to 10-15cm.

Drought resistant and suitable for arid ground although regular watering (every 3-5 days at the height of Summer) is beneficial. Produces insignificant yellow-green flowers in the Summer that are incapable of yielding seed in Mediterranean climates. Sowing May or September, with division in April or October. Apply organic fertilisers as chemical alternatives tend to cause damage. Sold commercially as sods.

SP. Hojita   FR. - GER. - IT.: *Dichondra*

63. *DIOSMA ERICOIDES (Diosma hirsuta, Diosma rubra)*

S.Africa - R - *PERENNE* - II/VII - *FLOR PERFUMADA* *PLENO SOL* - (-5°C.) - *SOPORTA LA PROXIMIDAD DEL MAR*

Breath of heaven

Lovely plant, with a generally misty look, and pleasant perfume. Forms a vaguely rounded, extensively branched shrub some 30-90cm. tall with needle-like leaves that give off an intense aroma when rubbed. The small white flowers, petals tipped with pink, come singly or in small groups. The early flowering season is both profuse and long lasting. Suitable for permeable, neutral or slightly acidic soils. Drought resistant.

Interesting cover for rockeries and flowerbeds. Suitable for containers. «Sunset gold» is a variety with golden foliage.

Avoid excess humidity, prune in Autumn to maintain low and dense. Propagate by sowing in Spring, or cuttings in Summer-Autumn

SP. Brecillo FR. Buchu   GER. - IT.: *Diosma*

64. DIPLOPAPPUS FILIFOLIUS
(Aster filifolius, Felicia filifolia)

S.W.Africa - M ![SEMPERENNE] - II/V - ![PLENO SOL] ![TOLERA LA CAL] - (-5°C.) - ![SOPORTA LA PROXIMIDAD DEL MAR]

Shrub aster, Wild aster

Fairly vigorous bush, with drooping branches and shiny, light-green, acicular leaves resembling needles. Reaches a height of 80-90cm. and double the width. Highly thought of for its long-lasting but precocious flowering period when, for many weeks, the whole plant becomes covered, with vast numbers of lilac flowers. This may be repeated in Autumn, but with less vigour. Tolerates any well drained soil, even if calcareous and is resistant to drought. Suitable for containers.

Excellent cover for rocky gardens, dry slopes and walls where it has a tendency to hang. Best pruned after the Spring flowering. Leafy cuttings in Spring, semi-woody ones in Autumn.

SP. - FR. - GER. - IT.: *Diplopappus filifolius.*

65. *DIPLOPAPPUS FRUTICOSUS*

(Aster fruticosus, Felicia fruticosa)

S.W.Africa - M  - III/VI -   - (-5°C.) -

Aster bush

A vigorous shrub resembling heather, with zig-zaging woody stems and thick, linear, almost spathulate, glandular-punctate leaves. It grows to 100-120 cm., and has abundant, beautiful, long-lasting lavender-blue flowers which appear towards the end of Winter. It can flower again in Autumn.

Widely appreciated for the colour and earliness of its flowers, and also for its frugality and resistance in dry conditions. It is an ideal ground-cover for rock gardens and borders. It combines well with *Euryops chrysanthemoides, Artemisia, Cineraria maritima, Cistus* and *Coronilla*. It is suitable for containers.

This species prospers in any well-drained soil. It should be pruned annually at the end of flowering. Multiplication is by cuttings, soft-wood in Spring or semi-woody in Autumn.

SP. -FR. - GER. - IT.: *Diplopappus fruticosus.*

65

66.   *DISPHYMA CRASSIFOLIA*

S.Africa - R - [PERENNE] - IV/VI - [PLENO SOL] [TOLERA LA CAL] - (-4°C.) - [SOPORTA LA PROXIMIDAD DEL MAR] [MELIFERA] [TOLERA LA CONTAMINACIÓN DEL AIRE]

Disphyma

Magnificent plant forming carpets which should not be walked on, it can also hang in the form of a cloak. It forms excellent lawns which can be used to replace the more typical grass. Very resistant to drought to the point that, once established, it does not require watering. It accepts any soils and is very useful for forming soft green carpets or for rockeries, slopes and small or large dry zones. It is apt for pots and containers and produces beautiful pink flowers. It is easily and quickly multiplied by cuttings in April or September and these can be planted directly.

SP. Cabellera, cabellera de la reina FR. IT. GER. *Disphyma.*

67.　DROSANTHEMUM FLORIBUNDUM
(Mesembryanthemum floribundum)

S.Africa - R - ![PERENNE] - IV/VI - ![PLENO SOL] ![TOLERA LA CAL] - (-5°C.) - ![SOPORTA LA PROXIMIDAD DEL MAR] ![MELIFERA]

Pink ice plant

Excellent carpet plant which does not resist trampling; it is a rapid grower and flowers spectacularly. It can be used as a hanging plant with stems of several metres. Its long trailing stems with grey, succulent leaflets do not reach more than 10 cm. above the ground and are totally covered with pink flowers in Spring. It is a magnificent substitute for grass in areas where water is scarce and is probably the best dry area ground cover plant. It tolerates the driest, arid, poor soils and is ideal for covering large areas, planting about 3 individuals per m2.

Annually, in October, it should be thinned out to prevent the development of bald patches. It is easily and rapidly propagated, taking advantage of October cuttings, which can be planted directly. It is sometimes planted as forage.

SP. Rocío rosa FR. Grain de riz GER. Eiskraut IT. *Drosanthemum floribundum.*

68. *DROSANTHEMUM HISPIDUM*
(Mesembryanthemum hispidum)

S.Africa - R -  - III/IV - ⚙ ⚠ - (-6°C.) - 🐝

Ice Plant

Dense ground-cover plant whose brilliant flowers cover the whole plant in Spring. It reaches a height of about 20 cm and has fleshy, cylindrical light green leaves with bright pappillae; the stems are lightly hairy. It has abundant, deep pink, almost lilac flowers with silky highlights which add to their beauty. It is very resistant to drought and to poor, arid soils. It is ideal for greening and adding colour to rock gardens, slopes and any dry areas. It is usually planted at a density of 3 per m2 and is apt for pots and containers.

It appreciates an annual thinning in October when it can be easily propagated from cuttings.

SP. Rocío púrpura FR. Cheveux raides GER. Eiskraut IT. *Drosanthemum hispidum.*

69. DYCKIA BREVIFOLIA (Dyckia sulphurea)

Brasil - L - 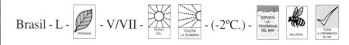 - V/VII - - (-2°C.) -

Dyckia brevifolia

Succulent, drought resistant bromeliad from the dry areas of Brasil. Grows as a dense, highly decorative mass of short, creeping stems and thick, heart-shaped leaves bordered with spines. The sulphur-yellow flowers appear in spikes on long slender stems. Vigorous and tolerant of all porous soils and long periods without water which is stored in thick roots.

Forms good, if slow growing, cover for small areas such as rockeries, amongst cactus and other low-maintenance succulents.

Division in April. Suitable for containers.

SP. - FR. - GER. - IT.: *Dyckia brevifolia*

70. *ECHEVERIA ELEGANS*

Mexico - L -  - III/VI - - (-4C°.) -

Mexican snowball, Hens and chickens

Pretty, succulent plant made up of dense, stemless rosettes and thick, light blue leaves with transluscent, white edges arranged like an artichoke. The coral-red and yellow flowers grow on curved pink stalks some 10-20cm. tall. Gows in the mountains of Mexico up to 3000m., being one of the most tolerant of the genus to low temperatures. Any soil with few nutritional requirements. Very resistant to drought.

Suitable as cover for small surfaces (requires patience) and for potting. Propagated from stolon or adult leaf cuttings (easily removed) or from shoots.

SP. Rosa de alabastro FR. -GER.- IT.: *Echeveria elegans.*

71. *ECHIUM FASTUOSUM*

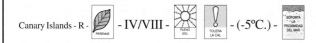

Canary Islands - R - [PERENNE] - IV/VIII - [PLENO SOL] [TOLERA LA CAL] - (-5°C.) - [SOPORTA LA PROXIMIDAD DEL MAR]

Viper's bugloss, Tower of jewels

Wonderful bush, wide and densly branched, with rosettes of large, rough, grey-green leaves around the stems. Produces compact, cylindrical inflorescences, 30-40cm. tall of a striking, intense blue. Suitable for poor, light, dry, even calcareous soils, in full sun or in half-shade under pine trees. A soil stabilising plant, good cover for slopes, rockeries and rustic gardens. Beautiful single, in clumps or with a sky or sea backround. Combines aesthetically with *Artemisia, Cistus* and *Hypericum* x «Hidcote».

Must be pruned lightly (sacrificing weak foliage) in April to promote the growth of new basal shoots. Withered flower spikes should also be removed. Cuttings from non-flowering terminal shoots in June-July.

SP. Taginaste FR. Vipérine GER. Natterkoff IT. Viperina.

72.   *ERICA GRACILIS*

S.Africa - M -  - IX/XII - - (-2°C.) -

Rose heath

Compact bush, some 40cm. high with linear leaves and prolific Autumnal flowers. Numerous lateral shoots carry 3-4 globular pink/purple flowers, 0.5cm long, from September to December, sometimes again in March. «Alba» is a pretty variety with white flowers. Accepts all, even calcareous, well drained soils. Tolerates periods of drought. Good cover for small, sheltered areas. Suitable for potting.

Requires only a light prune of the extremities after flowering but, in April, one third of the foliage should be removed to preserve the plants compact nature. Cuttings from lateral shoots in April. The late flowers make it a popular christmas potplant.

SP. Brezo rosa FR. Bruyère GER. Zierliche heide IT. Erica.

73. *ERIGERON MUCRONATUS*
(Erigeron karvinskianus, Vittadinia triloba)

Mexico - R - ![PERENNE] - IV/XII - ![PLENO SOL] ![TOLERA LA SOMBRA] ![TOLERA LA CAL] - (-7°C.) - ![SOPORTA LA PROXIMIDAD DEL MAR]

Fleabane

Graceful, herbaceous perennial, whose many thin, creeping branches form a rounded shrub some 30cm. high. The leaves are often trilobate. Produces abundant, pinkish-white, daisy-like flowers, 1.5cm in diameter, over a long period. A colonizing plant that reseeds spontaneously and can take over gardens.

Withstands drought but may temporarily lose its foliage until the Autumn during dry Summers. Tolerant of poor, arid, even calcareous soils. Good flowering cover for small and medium areas, slopes and rockeries where it combines well with many other species. Has potential fire-resistant qualities. Best planted at a density of 5/m2. Leaves drop at –8°C. but the plant survives down to –11°C. Easily propagated from cuttings taken in October or March.

SP. Vitadinia, Hierba pulguera FR. Vergerette GER. Feinstrahl IT. Erigero.

74.   *ERIOCEPHALUS AFRICANUS*

S.Africa - R - [PERENNE] - XI/III - [PLENO SOL] [TOLERA LA CAL] - (-5°C.) - [SOPORTA LA PROXIMIDAD DEL MAR] [TOLERA LA CONTAMINACIÓN DEL AIRE]

Eriocephalus

Attractive shrub up to one metre tall with grey, linear, aromatic leaves somewhat similar to rosemary. Small but abundant white, daisy-like flowers with brown centres and strange, woolly fruit that are surprisingly decorative. Has ornamental value throughout the year but especially in Winter. Fine in any permeable soil whether arid, stony or slightly basic. Drought resistant.

Used in clumps as cover for small and medium areas of rockeries and slopes. Good combined with *Ceanothus, Cistus, Grevillea, Rosmarinus, Teucrium,*etc. Can be grown as a low hedge as it tolerates heavy pruning in September and October. Cuttings in August.

SP. -FR. -GER. -IT.: *Eriocephalus.*

75.   *EUONYMUS FORTUNEI* 'Coloratus'
(Euonymus radicans 'Coloratus')

China - M -  - V/VI -

Purple-leaf Winter creeper

Loose, vine-like creeping shrub up to one metre tall with small (3-5cm. long), toothed leaves which turn pinky-purple at the start of Winter. The greenish flowers are insignificant but the abundant 1cm. wide, white and orange fruit are quite decorative. Best used as cover for flat areas, both large and small, side-slopes and rockeries. Best planted 3/m2. Prefers fresh, but will grow in any soils.

Erect branches must be removed in April and October to encourage creeping. Easily grown from cuttings taken in August and September. Tolerates light shade.

SP. Bonetero rastrero FR. Fusain GER. Plaffenhütchen IT. Evonimo.

76. *EUONYMUS FORTUNEI* 'Emerald and Gold'
(*Euonymus radicans* 'Emerald and Gold')

China - M -

Spindle tree

This recent, american cultivar forms excellent cover and is one of the most attractive spindle tree varieties especially in Winter when the golden yellow variegated leaves take on pink and bronze hues. Attractive and vigorous, low - growing , (up to 1.5m.) with curved shoots.

A stand of «emerald and gold» lights up any garden on even the dullest days, contrasting well with green foliage. Tolerates all types of cool soil, ideal for covering both large and small areas. Erect stems should be pruned in Spring and Autumn to encourage creeping. Cuttings root easily, and should be taken during the Summer.

SP. Bonetero rastrero FR. Fusain GER. Plaffenhütchen IT. Evonimo.

77.   *EUPHORBIA BIVONAE*

Sicily, N.Africa - L - [PERENNE] - III/V - [PLENO SOL] [TOLERA LA CAL] - (-5°C.) - [SOPORTA LA PROXIMIDAD DEL MAR] [TOLERA LA CONTAMINACIÓN DEL AIRE]

Euphorbia bivonae

Beautiful but little known species, named after the Sicilian botanist Bivona-Bernardi (1774-1837). An attractive, blue-grey shrub, rigid and extensively branched up to 1m. The stiff leaves and harsh tone give *bivonae* an almost metallic look. Unexpectedly produces lovely, abundant red-yellow flowers in the Spring.

Ultra-resistant to drought. Tolerates all porous soils and salty ground close to the sea. Useful low-maintenance cover for succulent gardens, coastal rockeries, dry slopes and for contrast with many blue and red flowering plants. Seeds can be germinated but only with a good deal of patience.

SP. -FR.- GER.- IT.: *Euphorbia bivonae*.

78.   *EUPHORBIA PULCHERRIMA (Poinsettia pulcherrima)*

S.W. Mexico - R [SEMIPERENNE] - XII/III - [PLENO SOL] - (-l°C.)

Christmas star, Mexican flame-leaf

Popular christmas pot-plant, striking in the garden because of its exotic looks. Survives in the most sheltered corners of some gardens with little frost. Forms a densly branched bush 2-3m tall, with milky sap and pretty, tender, green leaves. These are lost in the cold, if the plant is disturbed and after flowering. A short day plant which flowers when there are 10 hours of light and 14 of dark with night time temperatures of 18°C. (Christmas in the tropics). Keeps its leaves and may flower if the Autumn is mild.

Requires a strong prune in April to keep it dense and to improve flowering. Cuttings in June, which must be healed in cold water. The latex is medicinal and leaves, shoots and flowers can be eaten as a vegetable. Grows in any well-drained fertile soil.

SP. Flor de pascua, Nochebuena, Estrella de navidad, Flor de fuego, Estrella federal, Papagallo, Cardeal, Catalina FR. Etoile de Noël GER. Weihnachtsstern

IT. Stella di natale.

79. *EURYOPS CHRYSANTHEMOIDES*
(Gamolepis chrysanthemoides)

S.Africa - R -  - II/VI y IX/XII -  - (-7°C.) -

Daisy bush

   Rounded, densly branched bush up to 1m. tall with incised green leaves and a lengthy Spring flowering period, repeated in Autumn. Accepts all permeable soils prefering low alkalinity. Resistant to drought but benefits from occasional watering.

   Good, fast-growing, voluminous cover, especially when in flower. Highly adaptable, planted singly, in clumps or in combination with any number of other plants. Best used in rustic gardens. Suitable for containers. Kept compact by pruning after the Spring flowering. Tender cuttings, from shoots without flowers, root easily

SP. Margaritero verde   FR. -GER. - IT.: *Euryops chrysanthemoides*

80. *EURYOPS PECTINATUS (Gamolepis pectinatus)*

S.Africa - R - [PERENNE] - X/III - [PLENO SOL] - (-8°C.) - [SOPORTA LA PROXIMIDAD DEL MAR]

Resin bush

Woody, rounded shrub up to 1.5m high with attractive grey foliage and pretty Winter flowers. Dormant in the Summer. Incised, grey-green velvety leaves and numerous golden-yellow daisies, 5cm. in diameter, from the end of September to the beginning of April.

Accepts any well drained soil as long as it is not too basic. Tolerates long periods of drought but occasional Summer watering is advisable.

Useful, all round, fast-growimg, if voluminous ground cover. Suitable for containers. A cosmetic April pruning maintains density and is the perfect time to take tender cuttings from flowerless shoots.

SP. Margaritero gris   FR. -GER. -IT.: *Euryops pectinatus*

81.　*FELICIA AMOENA (Felicia pappei, Aster pappei)*

S.Africa - R -  - VI/XII -   - (-7°C.) -

Bush felicia

Attractive flowering perennial, some 40cm. high with thin, semi-succulent, shiny-green leaves, somewhat aromatic when crushed. Produces numerous, delicate blue flowerheads at intervals between June and December. Often confused with the similar species, *Agathaea coelestis*. Drought resistant but benefits from occasional Summer watering. Thrives in all, even calcareous soils. There are several cultivated varieties.

Excellent cover for small and medium areas, slopes and rockeries. Combines well with many other parallel flowering perennials. Cuttings will take root at any time except the Winter. Ideal for potting.

SP. Felicia　　　　　　　　　　　　　　FR. -GER. -IT.: *Felicia amoena*

82. *FESTUCA GLAUCA (Festuca ovina* 'Glauca')

Europe - R - 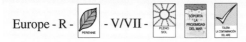 - V/VII -

Blue fescue

   Highly ornamental grass with fine, rigid, greyish-blue leaves forming dense mats some 20cm. tall. Produces elegant spikes of flowers at the beginning of Summer. Withstands even the poorest, aridest, most inhospitable soil with drought actually accentuating its blue colouration.
   Interesting grassy cover, tolerant of trampling, for small and large surfaces, rockeries, slopes and as a border for taller plants. Planted at a density of 10/m2. Blends well with bronze-tinged plants and blue or red flowers. Its texture contrasts with most other vegetation. Suitable for potting. Plants easily divided in Autumn and Spring.

SP. Cañuela azul FR. Fétuque bleue GER. Schafschwingel IT. *Festuca glauca.*

83.   *FRANKENIA LAEVIS*

Temperate coastal zones -R - ▨ PERENNE - V/IX - ☼ PLENO SOL - ⚠ TOLERA LA CAL - (-7°C.) - ▨ "SOPORTA LA PROXIMIDAD DEL MAR"

Sea heath

Interesting herbaceous perennial, low and caespitose, which forms exceptional, dense cover as its creeping stems advance and root. Average height is only 3-5cm. Heather-like leaves are compact and persistent, turning from grey-green to a pretty red during cold Winters. The tiny (5mm.) pink or purple flowers appear irregularly over large areas. Without doubt the best alternative to traditional grass in Mediterranean areas: withstands trampling, grows rapidly and does not need mowing. Also suitable for slopes. Prefers light, dry soil and is resistant to drought and the proximity of the sea. Planted at 7/m2.

Damaged by excess humidity, which first causes the leaves to redden and then an overall yellowing. Easily propagated from Spring and Autumn cuttings. Sold commercially as turf.

SP. Brezo de mar, Hierba sapera FR. Frankénie GER. Seeheide IT. Frankenia.

84. *GAULTHERIA REPENS (Gaultheria procumbens)*

USA - L - - VI/VIII -   -

Teaberry, Wintergreen

Small (15-20cm.), prostrate shrub, decorative and vigorous, suitable for carpeting the shaded areas of a garden. The shiny, dark green, oviform leaves some 4cm. long have toothed edges and grow grouped together at the tips of branches which turn a pretty pink in Winter. The small (1cm. wide), bell-shaped pink or white, waxy flowers come in small, terminal racemes. In Autumn the plant is covered in striking, bright scarlet fruit, similar to small, ornamental plums which last well into the Winter. Suitable for cool areas with sandy, acidic and peaty soil. Excellent cover in mountain gardens with minimum temperatures of -5°C . but must be planted on north-facing sites at low altitudes. Suitable for small areas, rock gardens and copses. Only needs light, tidying pruning. Sown in October, with cuttings in August and division in March. The fruit are edible and are a source of food for birds such as partridges. A stimulating infusion is made with the leaves.

SP. Ebúrnea FR. Petit thé des bois GER. Rebhuhnbeere IT. *Gaultheria repens.*

85.   *GAURA LINDHEIMERI*

Louisiana, Texas - R - - V/X -

Gaura

Erect, perennial shrub with green, purple tipped, spear-shaped leaves with wavy edges. The basal leaves are very persistent while the graceful, butterfly-like flowers, white turning to pink, some 4cm. across, appear profusely for many months. Tolerant of all porous soils and a degree of humidity. Resists both drought and cold. Spontaneous reseeding makes it a good colonizer of degraded land. Also useful, planted en masse, for low maintenance Mediterranean gardens, where the long flowering period makes it excellent cover for both small and large areas. The dense, but on the other hand, light flowers open up otherwise crowded compositions and fill up gaps in flowerbeds. Planted at a density of 3/m2. Suitable for containers. Easily propagated from seed and division in Autumn and Spring and from semi-woody cuttings in the Summer. Prune hard, almost down to the ground at the end of Winter.

SP. Gaura, Mariposilla   FR. - GER. - IT. :*Gaura*

86. *GAZANIA RIGENS (Gazania splendens)*

S.Africa - R - ![PERENNE] - IV/VII - ![PLENO SOL] ![TOLERA LA CAL] - (-5°C.) - ![SOPORTA LA PROXIMIDAD DEL MAR] ![TOLERA LA CONTAMINACIÓN DEL AIRE]

Treasure flower

Low vigorous creeper which forms dense carpets of green leaves with grey undersides, that temporarily becomes a sea of flowers. Flowerheads are yellow or orange with the bases marked with black and white. A sun worshipper, the flowers not opening on cloudy days, let alone in the shade. There are numerous varieties, some with iridescent flowers. Thrives in any fertile, well drained soil. Withstands drought but fortnightly watering during dry periods improves the flowering. Damaged by excess humidity.

Beautiful cover for large and small areas, combining well with *Lampranthus* and *Verbena*. Prevents the advance of fire. Short-lived, needing to be replaced every 4-5 years by cuttings taken in Autumn.

SP. Gazania FR. Gazanie raide GER. Gazanie IT. Gazania

87. *GREVILLEA JUNIPERINA (Grevillea sulphurea rubra)*

Australia - R -  - III/VII - (-7°C.) -

Juniper grevillea

Ample, ornamental bush between 1.5-2m. high with fine foliage and pretty flowers: The leaves are sharp, bright-green and linear while the showy, red flowers collect into feathery or spidery racemes along the two year old branches. The *sulphurea* variety has white flowers. Tolerates poor, dry soils but requires acidity.

Good cover if kept low and dense through pruning. Combines wonderfully with *Coronilla, Echium* and *Teucrium fruticans*.

To protect the flowers, pruning in two stages, April and October, is recommended. Erect branches must be removed or supressed to maintain a dense, compact specimen and to balance the irregular foliage. Lateral heeled cuttings are taken in July, and need to be treated with rooting powder. The pollen-laden flowers attract certain birds.

SP. - FR. - GER. - IT.: *Grevillea juniperina.*

88. *GYPSOPHILA REPENS*
(Gypsophila dubia, Gypsophila prostrata)

Europe - M - ![SEMPERENNE] - V/VII - ![PLENO SOL] ![TOLERA LA CAL]

Creeping baby's breath

    Caespitose little plant which forms a dense flowering carpet 20-25cm. tall. The stems are prostrate, later growing upright but supported by the nodes. Leaves linear, grey-green and somewhat succulent. Flowers abundant, 1cm. in diameter with a white or pink corolla. Withstands drought and grows in any, preferably calcareous fertile, porous soil. «Rubriflora» has intense red flowers.

    Very useful as a carpet for small surfaces; rockeries, slopes, paved areas and walls with calcareous mortar. Beautiful hanging over a wall and alongside rocks. Also combined with small perennials (*Brachcome, Dianthus, Diascia, Aubrieta, Bacopa,* etc). Propagate by seed sown directly onto the soil in April, or by tender cuttings also in April.

SP. Alborada FR. Gypsophie GER. Gypskraut IT. Gissofila.

89.   *HEBE* 'Autumn Glory' *(Veronica* 'Autumn Glory')

Hybrid - R - [PERENNE] - IX/XII y V/VI - [PLENO SOL] [TOLERA LA SOMBRA] - (-9°C.) - [SOPORTA LA PROXIMIDAD DEL MAR] [MELIFERA] [TOLERA LA CONTAMINACIÓN DEL AIRE]

Speedwell

A suposed hybrid between *Hebe x fransiscana* and *Hebe pimeloides*, both from New Zealand. A small, 60cm. bush, widely spread with reddish stems and small, dark green, rounded leaves which turn a violet-bronze in Autumn. Beautiful terminal spikes of intense purple flowers, appearing in Autumn and again in Spring. Tolerates all soils but prefers them light, fresh and fertile. Withstands drought but benefits from periodical summer irrigation.

Useful cover for rockeries and flowerbeds in coastal gardens. Suitable for containers. Kept compact through an annual April pruning. Cuttings from non-flowering shoots during the Summer. Attracts butterflies. Combines well with *Coronilla glauca, Euonymus Fortunei* «Emerald and Gold» and *Cuphea micropetala*.

SP. Verónica FR. Véronique GER. Ehrenpreis IT. Veronica.

90.   *HEBE* 'Carl Teschner' *(Veronica* 'Carl Teschner'*)*

Hybrid - R - 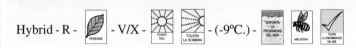 - V/X - - (-9°C.) -

Speedwell

Small cushion up to 40cm. high and 80cm. across, with highly ornamental leaves and flowers. Leaves are dark grey-green, while the short, fat racemes of flowers are violet-blue. Accepts all fresh, fertile soils and withstands drought and low atmospheric humidity.

Suitable as ground cover, for rocky gardens and in flowerbeds. Suitable for containers. Combines harmoniously with *Hemerocallis* and *Lobelia laxiflora* and with *Hebe* «Wiri Charm». Needs a light cosmetic prune in April. Tender cuttings from flower-less shoots during the Summer. Attracts butterflies.

SP. Verónica FR. Véronique GER. Ehrenpreis It. Veronica.

91.   *HEBE x FRANCISCANA* 'Variegata'
(Veronica x franciscana 'Variegata')

Horticultural - M - - VIII/XII y IV/VI - - (-9°C.) -

Speedwell

Hybrid between New Zealand's *Hebe elliptica* and *Hebe speciosa*, widely cultivated for its ornamental, variegated foliage. Rounded, compact and extensive with the leaves streaked with cream. Produces, throughout the year, numerous short, tight racemes of bright, violet, flowers which age to white. Grows up to 70cm. tall and 1.30m. wide. Extremely robust, weathering both wind and drought although regular Summer water is appreciated. Will thrive in any fresh, fertile soil. Tolerates shade but loses the beauty of its foliage. Suitable for containers. «Blue Gem», with green leaves and violet-blue flowers is widely cultivated. «Latifolia» has wide leaves and mauve flowers.

Lightly prune in April, and green shoots should be removed as soon as they appear. Cuttings from tender, flowerless shoots in the Summer.

SP. Verónica matizada FR. Véronique GER. Ehren preis IT. Veronica.

92.　*HEBE* 'Wiri Charm' *(Veronica* 'Wiri Charm')*

Horticultural - R - - VII/XI -  - (-8°C.) -

Speedwell

Modern hybrid, highly thought of for its dense, spreading growth, useful for covering the ground, and its attractive flowers. Low, 40cm. high, densly branched with pretty, elongated, dark green leaves and pretty, pink-purple flower spikes. Healthy and resistant to disease. Requires fresh, fertile soil and does not tolerate drought. Suitable for containers. Interesting in monochromatic flowerbeds or combined with groups of *Abelia* x *grandiflora* «Prostrata», *Centaurea candidissima, Ceratostigma griffithii* and *Gaura lindheimeri.*

Light cosmetic prune in April. Cuttings in the Summer, from non-flowering shoots. Attracts butterflies.

SP. Verónica FR. Véronique GER. Ehrenpreis IT. Veronica.

93.   *HELICHRYSUM PETIOLARE*
(Helichrysum petiolatum, Gnaphalium lanatum)

S.Africa - R - [PERENNE] - VII/IX - [PLENO SOL] - [TOLERA LA CAL] - (-5°C.) - [SOPORTA LA PROXIMIDAD DEL MAR]

Licorice plant

Pretty, but seldom seen ground covering creeper with highly ornamental foliage. Rounded, fleshy leaves are soft, silvery and furry while the Summer flowers are cream-white but of little decorative value. Grows in the most inhospitable soil provided it is well drained. Withstands drought and a certain degree of damp. Useful for rockeries, slopes and as a ground-covering mass. Particularly decorative combined with *Cistus, Rosmarinus, Scaevola* and *Teucrium*. Suitable for containers. A variety exists with golden foliage.

Prune lightly in Spring and Autumn to maintain compact. Propagation from parched cuttings. The furry leaves give immunity to disease.

SP. Siemprevivo FR. Immortelle GER. Kooigoed IT. Semprevivo.

94. *HELXINE SOLEIROLII*
(Parietaria soleirolii, Soleirolia soleirolii)

Corsican - R -  - (-4°C.) -

Baby's tears, Japanese moss, Corsican curse

Wonderful mossy carpet, formed by tiny, rounded leaves some 5cm. thick growing close together. Vigorous despite its delicate appearance. Can grow hanging from or climbing walls. Tolerates drought but its appearance improves if watered regularly throughout the Summer. Excellent carpet for small shaded areas; rockeries, copses, humid corners, alongside ponds and between flagstones. Planted at a density of 5/m2. Can be mown if irregular growth occurs. The leaves freeze at –5°C. but sprout again in the Spring as long as Winter temperatures do not drop below –12°C. Easily propagated from handfuls of cuttings in Spring or Autumn. Suitable for potting.

SP. Parietaria, Madre de mil GER. Bubiköpfchen heimglüch GER.-IT.:*Helxine soleirolii*

95. HEMEROCALLIS FLAVA *(Hemerocallis lilio-asphodelus)*

Asia, Europe - R - - V/VII -

Lemon day lily

Robust, rhizomatose shrub which is constantly expanding. Herbaceous with long, thin, arched leaves (some 70cm. long). The delicate, ephemeral, lemon-yellow flowers with their strong lily-like perfume last only one day and appear between May and July, or sometimes in the Autumn. There are clones of varying colours. Accepts any soil but the optimum is fresh and rich in humus. Tolerates both damp and drought.

Excellent cover for slopes, rockeries and flowerbeds; very attractive alongside water or a flowering *Ceanothus*. Combines well with the *Hebe*. Withered flowers must be removed to stimulate further blooming. Dry flower stems should also be removed. The dense root masses should be divided every three years, during the Spring or Autumn, again to maintain the number of flowers. Acts as a refuge for snails, which may attack tender shoots. Flower buds, picked the day before they open, are delicious in salads.

SP. Azucena efímera FR. Lis d'un jour GER. Taglilie IT. Giglio diurno.

96.   *HEUCHERA SANGUINEA*

Arizona, Mexico - M - [PERENNE] - V/VII - [PLENO SOL] [TOLERA LA SOMBRA] [SOPORTA LA PROXIMIDAD DEL MAR]

Coral bells

Elegant, cushion forming plant some 30cm. high with large, pretty, almost heart-shaped, dark green leaves. Produces bunches of bright red, bell-shaped flowers on the end of thin, rigid stalks. Ther are numerous varieties with pink and white flowers. Tolerates soils of varying quality, except those with excess clay. Tolerates drought but occasional irrigation extends the flowering period.

Good as cover for small areas and combined with other flowering perennials. Plant at 9/m2. Suitable for potting and a good source of cut flowers. Remove withered flower stalks and prune down to a third of its height in April to improve flowering and density. Propagation by division in April and October.

SP. Coralito,   GER. Purpurglöckchen   FR. - IT.: *Heuchera sanguinea*

97. *HYPERICUM CALYCINUM*

S.E. Europe - R · [PERENNE] - VI/IX - [PLENO SOL] [TOLERA LA SOMBRA] [TOLERA LA CAL] [SOPORTA LA PROXIMIDAD DEL MAR] [TOLERA LA CONTAMINACIÓN DEL AIRE]

Aaron's beard, Rose of Sharon

Highly decorative dwarf, stoloniferous creeper up to 35 cm High. Foliage, elegant, bright green. The large flowers a luminous yellow with showy stamens. It is drought resistant and is indifferent to soil types and quality though it prefers fresh, sandy soils. This is a useful and highly appreciated plant as it forms fast-growing cover over medium and large areas and is frequently used to cover the ground between shrubs and other tall plants. It is usually planted at a density of 12/m2.

Llight pruning is needed in April if the leaves have been cold-damaged. It should be cut back to within a few centimeters of the ground every two years if it is to remain compact and under control. Propagation is by semi-woody cuttings in August. It can be affected by fungus diseases. Though it is not melliferous it produces abundant pollen and attracts bees.

SP. Hipericón rastrero FR. Millepertius GER. Johanniskraut IT. Rosa di Saron

98.   *HYPERICUM x* 'Hidcote' *(Hypericum patulum* 'Hidcote')*

Horticulture - R - - VII/X -

St. John's wort

Attractive shrub up to 1.5m. high, compact yet lax with long-lasting flowers. The leaves are attractive and the yellow-gold flowers up to 7 cm. accross have orange-tipped anthers. Sterile, does not produce fruits, and is originally possible a hybrid of *H. calcinum* with *H. forrestii* or even with *H. cyathiflorum* «Gold Cup». Tolerates all heavy soils, even calcareous ones as long as they are fresh and well-drained. Resists dry periods but benefits from occasional summer watering. Shall be pruned down hard in April to maintain its dense form. Used to form beautiful borders of grown cover. Propagated by semi-woody cutting in August. It is not a melliferous plant but attracts bees by producing abundant pollen.

SP. Hipericón FR. Millepertuis GER. Hartheu IT. Iperico

99. *IBERIS SEMPERFLORENS (Iberis florida)*

Iran - M -  - X/IV - [FLOR PERFUMADA] [PLENO SOL] [TOLERA LA CAL] - (-5°C.) - [SOPORTA X LA PROXIMIDAD DEL MAR] [TOLERA LA CONTAMINACIÓN DEL AIRE]

Candytuft

A small, dense, mound-forming plant some 50 cm. high , distinguished by its beautiful, long-lasting but precocious flowers and spathulate leaves. Although less resistant to the cold than the more popular *Iberis sempervirens*, it is still highly recommended for temperate zones. The abundant corymbs of pure white flowers are pleasantly perfumed. It thrives in almost any soil and is resistant to drought.

A pretty plant for rockeries and for forming flowering carpets and bedding. The attractive white flowers combine well with other perennials and the variety 'variegata' has pretty white-tinged leaves. Dead flower-heads should be removed to prevent seeding. Cuttings should be taken in Spring and should be kept initially in the shade. It makes a good pot plant.

SP. Carraspique blanco FR. Thlapsi de Perse GER. Scheifenblume IT. Iberide

100. IBERIS SEMPERVIRENS

S.Europe - M -  - III/V -

Evergreen Candytuft

A graceful, early-flowering plant which forms clumps between 20 and 30 cm. high. The leaves are linear and acute while the abundant umbelliferous bunches of silver-white flowers have a pleasant perfume. This plant is drought resistant and tolerant of all soil-types. Flowering normally begins in early March but may start as early as January. There are several cultivated varieties and this species is ideal for ground cover in small areas, for rockeries and for perennial flowerbeds. It requires drastic pruning after flowering to force a second blooming a few weeks later. This plant was used by the Ancient Greeks but its name comes from Iberia, the old name for Spain where it is extremely abundant.

SP. Carraspique plateado FR. Thlapsi GER. Schleifenblume IT. Iberide.

101. *IRIS x HYBRIDA*

Horticultural - R - -IV/VI-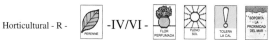

Flag Iris

Often classified incorrectly as *Iris germanica* or *Iris x germanica* and known horticulturally as *Iris barbata,* this is the tall garden Iris with large flowers. It arose from a series of hybrids of uncertain origin with many possible ancestors. It is an excellent soil-fixer due to its vigorous horizontal rhizomes. It is highly resistant to drought and prefers neutral to basic soils though it tolerates low acidity. Heavy damp soils should be avoided. The fragrant flowers come in a wide range of colours and in dozens of varieties. This plant is very useful as low-maintenance ground cover for rockeries, slopes and flowerbeds and combines well with most other plants. It must be planted with the rhizome close to the surface and is easily propagated by division after pruning back the leaves in Spring or Autumn. It is suitable for potting and the flowers are excellent for cutting and display. The rhizomes have medicinal properties.

SP. Lirio barbado FR. Iris des jardins GER. Schwertlilie IT. Iris.

102. ISOTOMA AXILLARIS
(Laurentia axillaris, Solenopsis axillaris)

Australia - R - [PERENNE] - VI/X - [PLENO SOL] - (-2°C.) - [SOPORTA LA PROXIMIDAD DEL MAR]

Isotoma axillaris

Graceful, herbaceous creeper growing up to 30-35 cm. It can be used as a hanging plant. The leaves are elongate and the beautiful, abundant and long-lasting inflorescences consist of blue tubular flowers, 3-4 cm. in diameter. It is highly resistant to drought but benefits from occasional watering during the flowering period. It accepts all healthy, well-drained substrates with a preference for rich, slightly acidic soils. It is an excellent pot-plant.

It is useful as ground cover and, when in flower, for giving colour to small areas It can be used in combination with *Armeria, Bacopa, Bidens, Centaurea candidissima, Centradenia, Dianthus, Diascia, Festuca, Oenothera etc.* And is propagated in Spring from seeds.

SP. Lorenza   FR. -GER. -IT.:*Isotoma axillaris*

103. *JACOBINIA SUBERECTA*

(Dicliptera suberecta, Justicia suberecta)

Uruguay - R -  - VI/X -  - (-4°C.) -

Jacobinia suberecta

Highly interesting, creeping perennial reaching a height of 50 cm. with a spectacular, long-lasting, Summer flowering-period. The leaves are oval, grey -green and velvety, and the resplendent bright orange tubular flowers are eye-catching on the end of tall flowering stems. This species ranks amongst the best, fast-growing ground-cover plants. It resists drought and thrives in all, even calcareous soils and in in humid, half-shady areas though in these it s leaves and flowers tend to lose their bright colours.

It is ideal for slopes and rockeries as well as cover for dry areas, both large and small.

It is usually planted at a density of 3 per m. sq. And is also suitable for potting. The leaves drop in cold periods but the plant survives down to –12°C. It attracts snails . Propagation is by cuttings taken in Spring or Autumn. The flowers contain large quantities of sweet nectar.

SP. Flamilla   FR. -GER. -IT.: *Jacobinia suberecta*

104. JUNIPERUS CHINENSIS
'Pfitzeriana Aurea'   *(Juniperus x media* 'Pfitzerana Aurea'*)*

Hybrid - M -

Golden Pfitzer Juniper

Resinous horizontal bush with attractive foliage, the branch tips taking on a pretty, golden hue in Summer and returning to their natural green in Winter. Adaptable to any permeable soil and resists drought. It is an excellent cover plant, much appreciated for small and medium-sized gardens due to its striking colour. It is widely used for flowerbeds, rockeries and slopes. New plants can be obtained from cuttings or layering in Autumn or by grafting. It is suitable for containers.

SP. Enebro rastrero FR. Genévrier de Chine GER. China-wacholder

IT. *Juniperus chinensis*

105. *JUNIPERUS CONFERTA* 'Blue Pacific'

Japan - M -

Shore Juniper

An attractive resinous bush up to 30 cm. tall with creeping stems up to 2 m. long. The foliage is blue-green when mature and apple-green in the juvenile state. It is tolerant of most conditions, even close to the sea but prefers permeable soils. It is very drought resistant.

This species provides excellent ground cover in dry areas and can be used on sloping terrain and in rock gardens. It is suitable for containers and is propagated by offshoots separated in Autumn, September cuttings or by grafting.

SP. Enebro tapizante   FR. -GER. -IT.: *Juniperus conferta*

106. *KALANCHOE BLOSSFELDIANA*
(*Kalanchoe globulifera* var. *coccinea*)

Madagascar - L - - I/IV - ☼ PLENO SOL - ⁑ TOLERA LA SOMBRA - (0°C..) - SOPORTA LA PROXIMIDAD DEL MAR - ✓ TOLERA LA CONTAMINACIÓN DEL AIRE

Christmas Kalanchoe

Popular and pleasing succulent pot plant which can only be grown outside in frost-free areas. It forms a compact plant some 30 cm. tall with fleshy, shining, dark green leaves with reddish borders. The whole leaf becoming deep red in Winter. The original, botanical species with scarlet flowers is rarely seen in cultivation. The horticulturalist's version of this plant has, however, a large number of colour varieties (white, pink, yellow etc.) often as the result of crossing it with *K. Flammea*. Dwarf varieties also exist.

This is a short-day plant requiring 13 hours of darkness to flower. It tolerates direct sun but prefers light or medium shade and grows in all types of soil but prefers acidic substrates. It is drought resistant and often has a second flowering period in the Autumn. It is useful when grown in groups forming highly attractive ground cover for small areas. Older plants can be rejuvenated by severe pruning and it is propagated from cuttings which should be taken in April and root easily.

SP. Escarlata   FR. - GER. - IT.: *Kalanchoe blossfeldiana*

107. KLEINIA MANDRALISCAE (Senecio mandraliscae)

S.Africa - M -  - (-5°C.) -

Kleinia mandraliscae

Carpeting succulent, valued for its drought resistance and its attractive bluish foliage which contrasts beautifully with the green leaves of other plants. It forms carpets about 15 cm thick which should not be trampled or trodden on. The fleshy leaves are cylindrical and the yellowish-white flowers resemble daisies.

Forms excellent ground cover for dry, arid terrain of all types and for slopes and rock gardens both large and small. It will share an area without becoming invasive and can be used with *Carpobrotus, Aptenia, Drosanthemum* and *Lampranthus*. Suitable for containers as it requires virtually no maintenance and is easily propagated from cuttings taken from Spring to Autumn.

SP. Bálsamo azul   FR. - GER. - IT.: *Kleinia mandraliscae*

108. *LAMIUM GALEOBDOLON*
'Variegatum' *(Lamiastrum galeobdolon* 'Variegatum', *Galeobdolon argentatum)*

Europe - R - [PERENNE] - V/VI - [TOLERA LA SOMBRA] [! TOLERA LA CAL]

Yellow archangel

Herbaceous evergreen reaching 20cm. in height, with long sterile suckers and substantial lateral growth. Leaves green with silver markings which take on a bronze hue in the Winter. The fertile runners have lemon-yellow flowers in the Summer months. This plant prospers in humid, fresh soils, preferably light and calcareous. Suitable for ground cover in shady parts of the garden, copses etc. It is usually planted at a density of 5 per M. sq. It can become invasive and is prone to attack by aphids. It is easily propagated by division in October and March and the tender young leaves are sometimes eaten in salads.

SP. Ortiga amarilla FR. Ortie jaune GER. Gold nessel IT. *Lamium galeobdolon*

109. LAMPRANTHUS AUREUS (Mesembryanthemum aureum)

S.Africa - M -  - II/V - - (-5°C.) -

Orange ice plant

Succulent with erect stems up to 30 or 40 cm. tall. The leaves are small, green and fleshy and the flowers a pretty bright orange. It is often confused with *L. aurantiacus* which has deeper orange-red flowers.

It forms beautiful cover for dry areas, planted at 5 per m.sq. It is very resistant to drought and accepts any type of porous soil even if rather calcareous. It is very useful for forming masses on rockeries and slopes and has a useful life of 3-4 years after which it can be easily replaced from cuttings taken in October. It is suitable for pots and containers.

SP. Mesem naranja FR. Ficoïde GER. Mittagsblume IT. Fiore di mezzogiorno.

110. *LAMPRANTHUS BLANDUS*
(Mesembryanthemum blandum)

S.Africa - R - ![PERENNE] - IV/V - ![PLENO SOL] ![TOLERA LA CAL] - (-6°C.) - ![SOPORTA LA PROXIMIDAD DEL MAR] ![TOLERA LA CONTAMINACIÓN DEL AIRE]

Pink ice plant

Succulent creeper, some 25 cm. tall with small fleshy leaves and dazzling pink flowers which contrast beautifully with those of other species. Often confused with the very distinct *L. roseus* which has simple, radiated ,darker pink flowers.

The flowering period lasts about three weeks with each flower lasting for a week. The flowers need sunshine and remain closed in the shade and on dull or cloudy days. This plant accepts all types of permeable soils and resists drought. It is useful cover for areas of rock garden, slopes and sunny areas and is suitable for pots and containers. Old flower-heads should be removed. Adult plants lose their ornamental value after 3 or 4 years but can easily be replaced from October cuttings.

SP. Escarchada FR. Ficoide GER. Mittagsblume IT. Fiore di mezzogiorno.

111. *LAMPRANTHUS SPECTABILIS*
(Mesembryanthemum spectabile)

S.Africa - R - [PERENNE] - V/VII - [PLENO SOL] [TOLERA LA CAL] - (-7°C.) - [SOPORTA LA PROXIMIDAD DEL MAR] [TOLERA LA CONTAMINACIÓN DEL AIRE]

Red ice plant

Succulent with thin, reddish, ground-hugging stems up to 25 cm. high and with very extensive growth. The blue-green fleshy leaves are about 1.5 cm. long, triangular in section and the surface is covered with transparent dots. The plant is totally covered with bright, showy red or purple flowers some 4-5 cm. in diameter. It is the most popular and widely grown garden mesemb. and is highly appreciated for its spectacular floration which, unfortunately only lasts about 3 weeks. A pink variety is sometimes seen.

It grows well in all porous soils and is excellent, drought resistant cover for rockeries, slopes and areas of arid stony ground. It is very spectacular when grown in large monochromatic masses. Plants must be replaced from cuttings every 3-4 years and withered flowers should be removed. Its high alkaloid content makes it toxic.

SP. Mesem rojo, Uña de gato FR. Ficoïde GER. Mittagsblume

IT. Fiore di mezzogiorno

112. *LAVANDULA ANGUSTIFOLIA*
(Lavandula officinalis, Lavandula spica, Lavandula vera)

Mediterranean - R - - VI/VIII -

English lavender, Common lavender

 A Mediterranean plant par excellence , 30-40 cm. high with greyish foliage and svelte lavender-blue flower stalks and heads. A plant of dry, basic soils which will adapt to most substrates if they are well-drained. The whole plant is delicately aromatic. A variety 'alba' has pure white flowers whilst 'rosea' produces pink blooms. Many beautiful hybrids have come about from a cross with *L. latifolia* : 'hidecote' (purple flowers), 'mustead' (blue flowers) etc.

 This species forms excellent bulk cover for rock gardens, slopes and arid terrain. It combines well with *Euryops, Malvastrum* and *Phlomis*. Withered flower-heads are best removed and plants should be pruned down to 15 cm. in March to keep them compact and prolong their useful life. The flowers attract butterflies and are said to repel mosquitos and greenfly and acts as a deterrent to clothes moths when placed in wardrobes. It is suitable for potting and should be propagated from cuttings taken in October. It has medicinal properties and is frequently used in the perfume industry.
SP. Espliego, Lavanda FR. Lavande vraie, Garderobe GER. Echter lavendel
IT. Lavanda.

113. *LAVANDULA DENTATA*

Spain, Portugal - R - [PERENNE] - II/III y VII/IX - [FLOR PERFUMADA] [PLENO SOL] [! TOLERA LA CAL] - (-7°C.) - [SOPORTA LA PROXIMIDAD DEL MAR]

Green lavender

Mat-forming bush up to 60 cm. tall with light green leaves with toothed, curved edges. It is a plant of exceptional florescence with short stems bearing light blue, perfumed flowers which appear, with short breaks, all the year round. There is a tall form (see photo.) with long peduncles and another 'candicans' with grey leaves and mauve to violet flowers.

It resists drought and thrives in all soils, prefering basic ones. It is a very useful ground cover forming clumps on slopes and in rock gardens and combines well with *Arctotis, Asteriscus, Centranthus, Eriocephalus, Phylica, Polygala* and *Santolina*. It is suitable for potting. Withered flowers should be removed at intervals and the bushes should be rounded off by pruning in April to rejuvenate them. It is easily propagated from cuttings taken in October. The strong aroma of this species repels greenfly and other insect pests and can be used to protect surrounding vegetation from attack.

SP. Espliego de jardín, Alhucema rizada, Cantueso dentado FR. Lavande
GER. Lavendel IT. Lavanda

114. *LAVANDULA PEDUNCULATA*
(Lavandula stoechas subsp. *pedunculata)*

Mediterranean - M - PERENNE - IV/VI - FLOR PERFUMADA - PLENO SOL - SÓLO SUELO ÁCIDO - (-8°C.) - SOPORTA LA PROXIMIDAD DEL MAR

Spanish lavender

Large, dense shrub with erect, branched stems and intensely fragrant, tomentose, greyish leaves with inrolled edges. It grows to 40-70 cm. high and the flowers come in wide, oval spikes which are quadrangular in cross-section and topped with a plume of large, blue-violet bracts. The spikes are borne on long peduncles, a character which distinguishes this plant from *L. stoechas*. In nature it is tolerant of the shade of pine forests.

A unique, decorative plant which is extremely resistant to drought and thrives, preferably, in acidic, siliceous soils. It forms good cover when grown in clumps, and is very attractive combined with *Cistus* and *Coronilla*. It is suitable for containers and is propagated by cuttings taken in October. It repels greenfly and other insects. It is used by the perfume industry and an infusion of the leaves has antiseptic properties and is used to clean wounds.

SP. Cantueso alado FR. Lavande papillon GER. Schopf-lavendel IT. Stecade.

115. *LEUCANTHEMUM OSMARENSE*
(Chrysanthemum hosmariense)

Marocco - M -  - IV/VII - - ! - (-9°C.) -

Leucanthemum osmarense

Wonderful little rhizomatous carpet plant, forming greyish cushions up to 20 or 30 cm. high. Leaves divided, with a silvery sheen. The flowers appear in early Spring but the decorative, scaly buds appear long before. The showy flowers are daisy-like with a yellow disc and have a peduncle some 15 cm. long.

The flowers may appear as early as February in favourable years. The species is highly appreciated for its rusticity, drought restistance, pretty foliage and ground-covering tendancies. It is useful for rock gardens, slopes and flower-beds especially amongst *Agathaea, Arctotis, Centranthus, Iris* and *Teucrium fruticans*. It is suitable for potting and is propagated by cuttings or division in April and October.

SP. Margarito   FR. - GER. - IT.: *Leucanthemun osmarense*

116. *LIMONIASTRUM MONOPETALUM*
(Limoniastrum articulatum)

Mediterranean - L -  - VI/VII -   - (-5°C.) -

Limoniastrum monopetalum

Shrub, between 75 and 120 cm. tall, with succulent, linear to spathulate, erect, greyish leaves. The attractive flowers are bright pink, turning pale violet as they shrivel.

This species will tolerate any soil even salty ones and is drought resistant. It is a good, low maintenance cover plant with its pretty colour contrasting with green. It forms attractive associations with *Bupleurum, Cistus, Diplopappus, Eriocephalus, Rosemarinus* and *Salvia microphylla*. It survives next to the sea and is suitable for containers. It is propagated from Summer cuttings and is a protected species in France. SP. Salado FR. Lavande de mer GER. Limoniastrum monopetalum IT. Limoniastrum monopetalum

117. LIPPIA REPENS
(Lippia canescens, Lippia nodiflora, Phyla nodiflora)

S.America - R -  - VI/IX -  - (-9°C.) -

Cape weed, Fog fruit, Daisy grass

Unbeatable ground-hugging cover forming carpets which are covered with tiny white, pink or lilac, butterfly-attracting flowers throughout the entire Summer. The tiny leaves are shed if the temperature falls below –5°C..

Very tough and resistant to drought. This species tolerates partial shade and is excellent for forming dense carpets in partial shade. It can be trampled without damage an will grow close to busy roads. It is suitable for covering paths and trails in gardens and is a good alternative for grass lawns in area where water is short. It is a useful ground stabilizer for slopes and rock gardens and is easily propagated from cuttings taken in Spring or Autumn and should be planted out at a density of 5 plants per sq. Metre.. The leaves can be eaten in salads.

SP. Bella alfombra   FR. Fraise de mer   GER. - IT.: Lippia repens

118. *LIRIOPE MUSCARI (Ophiopogon muscari)*

Japan - M - 🌿 - VII/XI - [SOMBRA] [TOLERA LA SOMBRA] [SOPORTA LA PROXIMIDAD DEL MAR] [MELIFERA] [TOLERA LA CONTAMINACIÓN DEL AIRE]

Big blue lily turf

Compact, rhizomatous mat up to 30 cm. tall made up of linear, dark green shiny leaves. It produces abundant, elegant, dark violet, bell-shaped flowers throughout the Summer and Autumn. These are formed on dense, erect spikes 8-12 cm. tall which emerge from between the leaves. The flowers are followed by black fruits. The *grandiflora* variety (in the photo) produces larger, lavender blue flowers.

Tolerates all soil types provided that they are not to basic. Resists drought although occasional waterings are appreciated. An excellent, tenacious cover plant for small areas. It is best planted at intervals of 40 cm. and is suitable for potting. Withered flower spikes should be removed to prevent seeding and old leaves should be removed in March. It is easily multiplied by plant division in March and April.

SP. Serpentina   FR. Barbe de serpent   GER. - IT.: *Liriope muscari*

119. *LIRIOPE SPICATA (Ophiopogon spicatus)*

China - M - - VII/IX -

Creeping lily turf

Vigorous, compact, rhizomatose plant which extends up to 40 cm.. the thin leaves are more or less erect and are about as high as the lilac-mauve spikes of flowers which are about 5-8 cm. long. It is suitable for all soil types and resists drought and direct sun as long as the soil is moist.

Invaluable cover for small areas in patios, copses and semi-shaded gardens. It should be planted at a distance of 45 cm. between plants and is suitable for potting. Withered flowers and dead leaves should be removed or pruned in March and propagation is by division of clumps in March-April or in October.

SP. Espigosa   FR. - GER. - IT.: *Liriope spicata*

120. *LITHOSPERMUM DIFFUSUM (Lithodora diffusa)*

S.W. Europe - R - V/VII -

Gromwell

Beautiful, evergreen creeper forming a dense carpet up to 20 cm. high which in Summer is covered in pretty blue flowers with a red or purplish sheen. The linear, hairy leaves are 2 cm. long and resemble those of Rosemary. The form 'alba' has white Spring flowers whilst 'heavenly blue' Is lower and more compact and bears abundant, delicate, gentian-blue flowers.

It requires well-drained, acidic soils and is an excellent cover plant for large surfaces, rock gardens and slopes. It combines well with *Asteriscus* and resists drought. It is suitable for potting. After flowering is complete, herbaceous cuttings can be taken from lateral shoots.

SP. Perlita, Litospermo FR. Grémil   GER. - IT.: *Lithospermum diffusum*

121. *LOBELIA LAXIFLORA* (*Siphocampylus bicolor*)

Mexico - R - [PERENNE] - V/XI - [PLENO SOL] [TOLERA LA SOMBRA] [TOLERA LA CAL] - (-4°C.) - [SOPORTA LA PROXIMIDAD DEL MAR] [TOLERA LA CONTAMINACIÓN DEL AIRE]

Lobelia laxiflora

A stoloniferous evergreen, forming dense, vigorous cover with abundant flowers. It reaches a height of between 60 and 90 cm. but is cut down at temperatures of –5°C. though the rootstock survives to –12°C. producing new growth in Spring. The leaves are narrow and elongated. Its flowers which are produced between Spring and Autumn are attractive and elegant. They are abundant, tubular and orange red in colour with a yellow throat.

This species grows in any rich, well-drained soil though it prefers calcareous substrates. It resists drought. It is an unbeatable cover plant whose cloudy effect is used to lighten up over-dense beds. It is a marvellous companion for *Agapanthus, Artemisia, Atriplex, Bupleurum, Centaurea pulcherrima, Chrysanthemum frutescens, Cineraria, Convolvulus argenteus, Echium, Felicia, Helichrysum, Teucrium fruticans etc.* Propagation is by division in April and new plantings should be at a density of about 3 per M sq.

SP. Indianita   FR. - GER. - IT.: *Lobelia laxiflora*

122. *LONICERA PILEATA*

China - M - ![leaf icon] PERENNE - V - ![full sun] PLENO SOL ![tolerates shade] TOLERA LA SOMBRA ![tolerates lime] TOLERA LA CAL ![tolerates sea proximity] SOPORTA LA PROXIMIDAD DEL MAR ![tolerates air pollution] TOLERA LA CONTAMINACIÓN DEL AIRE

Privet honeysuckle

Pretty, lustrous bush, 50-60 cm. tall, compact, flattened and spreading, almost carpet forming. It has small, oval - elongated, glossy leaves. The cream-white flowers grow hidden amongst the foliage and are followed by small, violet, translucent berries. It thrives in any soil rich in humus but prefers calcareous conditions. It resists periods of drought and tolerates the shade of open understories.

It is an efficient and elegant cover plant requiring low maintenance and is useful in all gardens and situations. It is disease free and is an up-to-date classic plant which can be used for containers. Propagation is from cuttings taken from mature stems in July and August.

SP. Brillantina FR. Chèvrefeuille à cupule GER. Heckenkirsche IT. Caprifoglio

123. *LOTUS CRETICUS (Lotus commutatus)*

Mediterranean - R 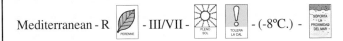 - III/VII - - (-8°C.) -

Lotus creticus

Leguminous dense, spreading, woody-based shrublet which forms attractive cover. The leaves are greyish and silky, almost silvery. The bright yellow flowers are abundant, they come in groups of 1-8 on stalks which are longer than the leaves. It is a lover of dry, sunny conditions and does not survive cold, Winter damp. It thrives in the most hostile conditions, even in salty soils and prefers basic substrates to acid ones. It can grow to between 20 and 40 cm.

It forms a useful, permanent cover for dry areas and is excellent for slopes and rockeries but it can also be grown as a hanging plant. It harmonizes well with *Agathaea*, *Arctotis, Felicia* and *Scaevola*. It is suitable for potting and is propagated from seed sown in Spring.

SP. Coronita, Cuernicillo de mar FR. Lotier de Crète   GER. - IT.: *Lotus creticus*

124. *LOTUS HIRSUTUS (Bonjeana hirsuta, Dorycnium hirsutum)*

S. Portugal - R -  - V/VIII -

Canary Clover

   The variety 'Frejorgues' which appears in the photo is a vigorous creeping shrub of high ornamental value which grows to 60 cm. tall. Its dense, layered vegetative growth completely suppresses the growth of small weeds. It has pretty whitish, downy leaves and white, pink-streaked flowers which appear abundantly throughout the year. It is unfussy about soil types but needs good drainage. It is very drought resistant.

   This plant forms excellent ground-cover for dry areas, rockeries and slopes. It is exceptional when used intermingled with other cover plants. It reseeds spontaneously and can be used to colonise and stabilise ground. It should be planted at a density of 2-3 per M.sq. It is sensitive to excessive damp. It requires a light, cosmetic, compacting pruning in September but will tolerate heavy cutting-back when necessary. It is propagated from Autumn or Spring cuttings.

SP. Bocha peluda, Hierba del pastor   FR. - GER. - IT.: *Lotus hirsutus*

125. *LYCHNIS CORONARIA (Agrostemma coronaria)*

S.Europe - R - - V/VII -

Crown pink

Highly decorative, tomentose,densely branched, evergreen which forms small wide mats of woolly, silver-grey leaves. Floriferous, the flowering stems reaching 60 cm with showy, intense purple, flowers about 3 cm. across. 'Alba' is a white-flowered form, 'atrosanguinea' red, and 'rosea' white with a.pink centre. It supports drought and prospers in all well-drained soils though it prefers basic conditions.

Widely used in flower-beds, rock-gardens and semi-wild areas in combination with other carpeting species. Plants should be bedded out at a distance of 25 cm. and are relatively short-lived so that gaps should be filled each year. It is suitable for potting. Dead inflorescences should be removed. It is propagated by direct sowing in September or by the separation of lateral shoots in March or April.

SP. Coronaria, Candelaria, Clavel lanudo FR. Coquelourde des jardines

GER. Kronen-Lichtnelke IT. Coronaria.

126. LYSIMACHIA CONGESTIFLORA

Tibet - R - [PERENNE] - V/VII - [TOLERA LA SOMBRA]

Lysimachia congestiflora

A pleasant, creeping evergreen with pretty bronze-grey leaves. The attractive yellow flowers have a darker centre and grow in dense clumps. This plant appreciates a shady site and, infull sun it does not flower or the young flowers are quicky burned up. It requires humid, clay soils and can grow up to 20 cm. tall.

It is useful as a cover plant for half-shaded areas and combines well with *Ajuga, Bacopa, Bergenia, Campanula, Centradenia, Clivia, Convallaria, Cymbalaria, Helxine, Lamium, Saxifraga, Tradescantia* and *Viola*. It is apt for pots and can be propagated by division in October or March.

SP. Flor del metro   FR. -GER. - IT.: *Lysimachia congestiflora*

127. LYSIMACHIA NUMMULARIA

Europe - R -  - V/VII - [PLENO SOL] [TOLERA LA SOMBRA]

Moneywort

Valuable creeping, carpeting plant which adapts to the contours of the terrain. It grows up to 15 cm. and the foliage forms as oft, attractive carpet which does not resist trampling. It can also be grown as a hanging pot plant. It produces abundant bright yellow flowers some 2 cm. in diameter. It is fairly adaptable but prefers humid,organic soils, rich in clay. It grows well in full sun provided the ground is fresh and it also prospers in half-shade. It should be watered periodically in drier areas. It does not impede weed growth .

It is excellent cover for both large and small areas, slopes and rockeries and is very pretty grown on walls or alongside water. The variety 'alba' has golden leaves but the colour is easily lost. Rooted stems can be separated in October and March. A decoction of the leaves has astringent, vulnerary and febrifuge properties.

SP. Hierba de la moneda, Monetaria FR. Herbe aux écus GER. Hellerkraut

IT. *Lysimachia nummularia*

128. *MALVASTRUM CAPENSE (Anisodontea capensis)*

S.W.Africa - R **[PERENNE]** - V/XI - **[PLENO SOL]** **[TOLERA LA CAL]** - (-7°C.) - **[SOPORTA LA PROXIMIDAD DEL MAR]** **[MELIFERA]**

Busy Lizzie

An extensively branched, glandular, half-woody, aromatic shrub up to 1 m. with delicate foliage and attractive flowers. It has small, dark green, rough leaves with 3-5 toothed lobules. The small flowers are similar to those of *Hibiscus*, light purple at the tips of the petals and darkening towards the centre. They appear all the year round but are most abundant in the Summer. This species does not have a resting period except in extremely cold conditions. It is undemanding and accepts all types of soil. It is drought resistant although periodic Summer watering is beneficial.

It forms good cover if kept dense by regular pruning of the new shoots. It comlines easily with other plants and is suitable for containers. It is freely propagated from cuttings. In excessively humid conditions it may be attacked by mildew (*Puccinia malvacearum*).

SP. Malvastro, Malva del Cabo   FR. - GER. - IT.: *Malvastrum capense*

129. *MELIANTHUS MAJOR*

S.Africa - R -  - V/VI -  - (-4°C.)

Honey flower, honey bush

A magnificent bush with a thick basal stem which divides into numerous branches bearing spectacular, exotic foliage. It grows to between 1.5 and 3.0 m. tall. The large (25-40 cm. long), curious leaves are fern-like and a pretty blue-green, they are silvery-grey when young . This plant produces terminal clusters (30 cm. long) of attractive red-brown flowers which secrete abundant nectar. The leaves produce an unpleasant smell when crushed.

It is drought resistant and forms highly ornamental cover when used on its own, in flowerbeds or combined with carpeting succulents to emphasize its foliage. It is best pruned almost to ground level in April to stimulate more vigorous growth and larger leaves. Propagation is from seed sown in the Spring or from cuttings taken from April to May and it thrives in fertile, permeable soils. It is used as a medicinal plant and is suitable for containers.

SP. Melero, Flor de miel

FR. - GER. - IT.: *Melianthus major*

130. *MYOPORUM PARVIFOLIUM*

Australia - R -  - VII/IX - - (-7°C.) -

Myoporum parviflorum

Known as 'Myoporum repens' by many horticulturalists this is a low creeping plant 25-40 cm. high the branches of which root at the nodes as they extend. It has pretty, glossy evergreen foliage of dense succulent linear leaves 1-3 cm. long. It produces small, star-like white flowers with an aroma similar to that of honey and tiny purple fruits. There are several varieties with pink flowers and different leaf-textures. It resists drought and tolerates half-shade. The species is used to prevent erosion and for its fire-proof properties. It grows in any permeable soil and is excellent and attractive ground cover and is widely used in California. It is suitable for slopes and rockeries of any size and can easily be propagated from Summer cuttings.

SP. Siempreverde   FR. - GER. - IT.: *Myoporum parviflorum*

131. NANANTHUS TRANSVAALENSIS
(Aloinopsis transvaalensis)

S.Africa, Transvaal - R - ![PERENNE] - X/V - ![PLENO SOL] ![TOLERA LA CAL] - (-5°C.) - ![SOPORTA LA PROXIMIDAD DEL MAR]

Nananthus transvaalensis

Interesting, pretty succulent which is fast-growing and has a long flowering period. It is difficult to find commercially and is consequently poorly represented in gardens. It has small, triangular leaves and abundant white flowers. It forms a contour-hugging carpet only a few cm. high and can be used as a hanging plant. It is extremely resistant to drought and to the proximity of the sea and thrives in any well-drained soil but prefers them calcareous.

It is suitable for covering dry soils, slopes and rock gardens. The colour of its flowers allows it to be used in combination with many other carpeting and creeping species and is also suitable as a pot plant. Easily propagated from cuttings taken in May or October.

SP. Enanillo   FR.- GER. - IT.: *Nananthus transvaalensis*

132. *NEPETA x FAASSENII*

Horticultural - R -  - V/IX - - - (-9°C.) - -

Catmint

Frequently but erroneously known as *Nepeta mussinii* this is a pretty, floriferous, aromatic plant some 40 cm. high with fine, silvery-grey leaves smelling pleasantly of mint. It produces abundant spikes of lavender-blue flowers and tolerates drought and poor, arid soils. 'Six hills giant' is a very vigorous form (50-60 cm. tall and 'snowflake' has compact stems and white flowers.

This is a highly ornamental cover plant used on rockeries and slopes and combines with *Bidens, Senecio, Saxifraga* and *Verbena*. Useful for large and small areas. The withered flower stems are best removed and a heavy pruning in early Spring encourages new growth. Plants should be replaced every three years using plants divided in March. It should never be transplanted in Autumn to prevent rotting. Like *Nepeta cataria* the true 'cat mint' this species is unpleasant for cats. It is suitable for planting in pots.

SP. Menta gris, Hierba gatera FR. Herbe-aux-chats GER. Katzenminze IT. Gataia, Erba gatta

133. *NEPHROLEPIS TUBEROSA (Nephrolepis cordifolia)*

Tropical Asia - R - -   - (-2°C.) - -

Erect sword fern, ladder fern

Stoloniferous fern with tubers at root-level which forms broad mats of erect fronds up to 60 cm. high. It resists drought and adapts to all soil types, prefering a fresh, humus-rich substrate and it will prosper in both full sun and shade although the best foliage is obtained in half-shade conditions. The leaves die back at –3°C. but the plant survives down to –7°C. with new shoots appearing after the Winter.

It is an impressive ground cover plant, highly ornamental grouped around rocks and tree trunks or combined with many other plants. It is suitable for potting and is easily propagated by division and from separated tubers.

SP. Helecho espada   FR. - GER. - IT.: *Nephrolepis tuberosa*

134. *OENOTHERA DRUMMONDII (Onagra drummondii)*

USA - R - [SEMPEREENNE] - VI/IX - [PLENO SOL] [TOLERA LA SOMBRA] - (-9°C.) - [SOPORTA LA PROXIMIDAD DEL MAR]

Evening primrose

An evergreen perennial with drooping branches which later straighten out to between 50 and 60 cm. 'Nana' in the photo is a dwarf form some 20-30 cm. tall. It is a highly decorative species with large (5 cm. diameter) lemon-yellow flowers with divided petals. These are short-lived, opening in the evening and withering by the morning after taking on a redish hue. The flowering period is , however, along one. Its deep roots make it a good soil stabilizer and it tolerates almost any type of permeable soil. It is drought resistant and can be damaged by excessive humidity.

It is particularly stiking when used as a ground cover in groups or mixed with clumps of *Agathaea, brachycome, Felicia, Scaevola* and*Verbena.* It should be planted at 4-5 per M. sq. And is usually propagated from seed or by plant division in April.

SP. Borriquera, Hierba del asno FR. Bergamote, Onagre GER. Nachtkerxe IT. Enotera.

135. *OPHIOPOGON JABURAN*

Japan - L - ![PERENNE] - V/VII - ![TOLERA LA SOMBRA] ![SOMBRA] ![TOLERA LA CONTAMINACIÓN DEL AIRE]

White lily-turf

Dense white bush 30-50 cm. tall with long, linear, hanging, multinerved, blunt leaves. The tiny pure white flowers are produced in short racemes on long procumbent stems. The oblong, glossy, violet-blue fruits are highly decorative. There are several varieties of this species in cultivation.

It accepts any type of soil and is relatively tolerant of drought. It is a useful cover plant for small shaded areas. To take full advantage of the ornamental fruit the old shrivelled flowers should not be removed. Old leaves should however, be removed in March. Easily propagated by division in Spring or Autumn, this species is suitable for use as a pot plant.

SP. Cintillas   FR. - GER. - IT.: *Ophiopogon jaburan*

136. *OPHIOPOGON JAPONICUS (Convallaria japonica)*

Japan - L -  - VI/VII -

Mondo grass, Lily-turf

Dense, grass-like plant with glossy, dark-green linear leaves which can reach a height of 20 cm. The rhizomes spread slowly and can produce very large colonies. It bears small, white, tender pink or light violet flowers which are followed by by small, curious porcelain-blue fruits about the size of a pea.

It tolerates drought but prefers regular watering and accepts any soil even calcareous ones. In cool sites it will tolerate full sun.

It is a good carpeting plant for wooded and shady areas and is a good lawn substitute in places where grass will not grow. It does not require cutting but survives trampling as long as it is regularly mown. It should be planted at a density of 7 per m. sq. And can be propagated by division throughout the year. The tubers are edible.

SP.Convalaria FR.Herbe aux turquoises GER.*Ophiopogon japonicus* IT. Ofiopagone

137. *OSTEOSPERMUM ECKLONIS (Dimorphotheca ecklonis)*

S.Africa - R - 🍃 *PERENNE* - II/VII - ☀️ *PLENO SOL* - ⚠️ *TOLERA LA CAL* - (-5°C.) - 🌊 *SOPORTA LA PROXIMIDAD DEL MAR*

Cape marigold

An erect bush, more or less prostrate, growing up to 1 m. high. The white flowers with blue undersides close up at night. It is suitable for all types of soil and is drought resistant. There are many varieties, one of them 'prostrata' is an interesting cover plant being lower growing than var. *ecklonis.*

Good forming covering beds with a variety of other species and it can be used as a fire-break border. It is suitable for containers. Withered flowers should be removed continuously and an October pruning compacts the plant if necessary. It is easily propagated from cuttings using tender flowerless shoots during April.

SP. Matacabras, estrella polar   FR - GER. - IT.: *Osteospermum ecklonis*

138. *OSTEOSPERMUM FRUTICOSUM*
(Dimorphotheca fruticosa)

S.Africa - R - [PERENNE] - I/V - [PLENO SOL] - [TOLERA LA CAL] - (-5°C.) - [SOPORTA LA PROXIMIDAD DEL MAR]

Trailing African daisy, Burgundy mound

Vigorous, low, spreading bush with long creeping stems reaching a height of 30-40 cm. Produces abundant violet flowers between January and May, occasionally with a second flowering in the Autumn. Unfussy about poor, arid and even calcareous soils as long as they are light. Tolerates long periods of drought. There are several varieties with white, pink and lilac flowers.

Excellent ground cover for small and medium areas, combining well with *Euryops*. It should be planted at a density of 3 per M. sq. And is suitable for containers. It is claimed that this species smothers fires. It can be pruned occasionally after flowering to compact the foliage and is easily propagated from flowerless cuttings in the Spring.

SP. Margarita del Cabo, Dimorfoteca   FR. - GER. - IT.: *Osteospermum fruticosum*

139. *OTHONNOPSIS CHEIRIFOLIA*
(Othonna cheirifolia, Hertia cheirifolia)

N.Africa - M - [PERENNE] - II/IV - [PLENO SOL] [TOLERA LA CAL] - (-6°C.) - [SOPORTA LA PROXIMIDAD DEL MAR] [TOLERA LA CONTAMINACIÓN DEL AIRE]

Othonnopsis cheirifolia

Pretty, creeping shrublet, densely branched with thick, semi-succulent, bluish foliage. It forms rounded bushes between 25 and 30 cm. high. The leaves are thick, spathulate and bluish green to silvery in colour. It has pretty, abundant lemon-yellow flowers borne in solitary heads, 2-3 cm. across. Flowers from February to the end of May with a possible second blooming in Autumn and Winter. Ages well and is drought resistant. Grows in any well-drained soil but prefers a calcareous substrate.

Forms interesting ground-cover on slopes and rockeries. Also hangs pleasantly from walls. It should be planted at a density of 5 per m. sq. And is apt for potting. It is easy to propagate from cuttings taken in Summer or by division in Spring.

SP. Azulín   FR. - GER. - IT.: *Othonnopsis cheirifolia*

140. *PACHYSANDRA TERMINALIS*

Japan - M -  - III/IV -

Japanese spurge

Lovely spreading shrub some 20 cm. high forming a dense carpet of highly decorative foliage. Its green, glossy leaves grow out from the tips of the stems bunched into a diamond shape. The small petal-less flowers are of little ornamental value and form small, greenish-white spikes. It prefers fresh, fertile soils but grows vigorously in most substrate types. It is tolerant of a certain degree of drought. The less vigorous form 'variegata' has the leaves striped and bordered with white.

This is a jewel of a plant which provides excellent cover for shady areas both wet and dry and large and small, it even grows in the deep shadow thrown by large trees. It should be pruned to within 6 cm. of the ground when the foliage loses quality with age. Propagated by plant division in March or woody cuttings in August or September. It is suitable for use as a pot plant.

SP. Diamante   GER. Ysander

FR. - IT. *Pachysandra terminalis*

141. *PELARGONIUM GRAVEOLENS*

S.Africa - R - PERENNE - V/X - PLENO SOL - TOLERA LA CAL - (-5°C.) - SOPORTA LA PROXIMIDAD DEL MAR - MELIFERA

Rose geranium

Diffuse, spreading branched shrub up to 90 cm. tall. The leaves deeply divided (palmatifid) and highly aromatic giving a strong scent of roses when bruised. It is often confused with *Pelargonium capitatum* (rose-scented storksbill) which has a milder, more pleasant scent. Thrives well in arid conditions and tolerates basic soils.

Interesting cover for dry areas, slopes and rock gardens. Except for a few varieties (photo) the pink flowers are of little ornamental value. It is suitable for potting and is freely propagated from cuttings in Spring and Summer. The edible leaves are used to repel mosquitoes and larvae harmful to other plants and commercial extracts are used in the perfume industry.

SP. Geranio de rosa FR. Faut géranium rosat GER. Rosengeranie IT. Pelargonium graveolens

142. *PEROVSKIA ATRIPLICIFOLIA*

Afghanistan - R -  - VII/IX -

Azure sage

A spreading, semi-woody shrub with a feathery appearance reminiscent of a giant lavender and a superb, late, florescence. It reaches a height of about 1.5 m. and the thin, deeply toothed, rhomboidal, greyish leaves are sticky to the touch and give off a strong aroma of sage. The lavender-blue flowers are borne in long spikes and the variety 'blue spike' in the photo has long spikes with pale blue flowers and finely cut leaves. It is about 1 m. tall and flowers from July to October. The species is drought resistant and grows in any well-drained soil.

It is a seasonal cover plant of great beauty which can be planted singly or in groups. It is suitable for lightening up the strong impact of dense flower-beds and combines well with other plants. It should be planted at a density of 2-3 per m. sq.. Withered flowers should be removed and the plant pruned down in March to within 20 cm. of the ground. It is propagated from tender cuttings in the Spring.

SP. Salvia rusa   FR. - GER. - IT.: *Perovskia atriplicifolia*

143. *PHALARIS ARUNDINACEA*
'Picta' *(Phalaris arundinacea* 'Variegata')

USA, Europe - R - - VI/VII -

Reed grass, Ribbon grass

Ornamental grass which forms dense, spreading, rhizomatous mats with large leaves with white borders. Its spreading, almost invasive growth makes it useful as ground cover and it is decorative due to the brightness of its foliage. Its cane-like stems, which can grow up to 1 m. tall, produce the typical terminal inflorescences of its family.

It is recommended for humid sites even in water and tolerates half -shade even though it loses colour and brightness. It withstands dry periods and should be planted at about 3 per m. sq. The dried, semi-mature inflorescences are used as permanent decorations. Once a year pruning in March helps to keep the plants low and attractive but impedes flowering. It is propagated by division in March and is sometimes cultivated as a forage plant for grazing. The seeds are similar to canary seed and are greatly appreciated by birds.

SP. Hierba cinta, alpiste de forraje FR. Roseau GER. Militz, rohrglanzgras IT. Erba, bindella falaride.

144. PHLOMIS FRUTICOSA

S.Europe - R -  - IV/VII -

Jerusalem sage

Shrub up to 1.5 m. with large, velvety leaves which are greyish-green above and white-grey on the undersurface. It has pretty, golden yellow flowers and is suitable for any well-drained soil even if poor, dry and calcareous.

It forms interesting cover with contrasting foliage and its beautiful, always frugal flowers are second to none. It is very useful as a solitary specimen plant or as a bedding plant. It should be planted at a density of 1 per m.sq. and can be drastically pruned in March and withered flowers and weak shoots should always be removed. It is propagated by seed or cuttings during the Summer.

SP. Salvia amarilla, Orejas de burro, Salvia de Jerusalén   FR. Sauge de Jérusalem
GER. Jerusalem-salbei   IT. *Phlomis fruticosa.*

145. PHLOX SUBULATA (Phlox setacea)

USA - R - - IV/V -

Creeping phlox , Moss phlox

   Herbaceous carpeting plant with acute, linear leaves about 2 cm. long which can form dense, floriferous turf. The diffuse, creeping stems are covered with small flattened flowers in groups of 2-4. Flower colour is variable according to the variety (pink, lilac, white, blue, lavender or purple-red), all having a darker centre. It grows well in diverse soils but prefers them light, fresh and humus-rich. It only grows to 5-15 cm. tall.

   An ideal carpet for rockeries and in front of mixed beds. It is useful for sheltered slopes with little sun and for large or small areas. It should be pruned after flowering. It is propagated from basal-shoot cuttings taken in July or from sections of underground stems in March. It can also be multiplied by division in Spring and Autumn. Plants are suceptible to attack by slugs.

SP. Flox musgo FR. Phlox mousse GER. Flammenblume IT. Fiamma.

146. *PHYLICA ERICOIDES (Phylica glabrata)*

Horticulture - [PERENNE] - X/V - [PLENO SOL] - (-5°C.) - [SOPORTA LA PROXIMIDAD DEL MAR]

Sage

Attractive, robust hybrid between two red-flowered Mexican species. It is a mass of diffuse branches which forms a round bush up to 90 cm. tall. The small elliptical leaves have a minty aroma and abundant red-purple flowers are produced from May to October and even throughout the Winter in mild conditions. There is a variety with pink flowers (see photo). It is drought resistant and grows in all types of well-drained soil.

Valuable cover for extensive areas , forming large masses. The shoots are unpredictable, tending to grow erratically so that the plants should be pruned two or three times a year. This stimulates flowering. A severe pruning in March maintains compactness. It should be planted at a density of 3 per m.sq. and is propagated from Spring cuttings. The flowers contain delicious nectar.

SP. Salvia gremi FR. Sauge GER. Salbei IT. Salvia.

147. *PITTOSPORUM TOBIRA* 'Nana'

China - M -  PERENNE -IV/VI - FLOR PERFUMADA | PLENO SOL | TOLERA LA SOMBRA | ! TOLERA LA CAL | - (-9°C) - SOPORTA LA PROXIMIDAD DEL MAR | TOLERA LA CONTAMINACIÓN DEL AIRE

Mock orange

A pretty form of the species *Pittosporum tobira* which is small, round and compact, growing up to 1 m. tall and 2 m. across. It has attractive, glossy, dark-green, heart-shaped leaves. The creamy-white flowers appear in Springtime and have a strong scent of orange blossom. It adapts well to all soils but clay and lime are best avoided. It thrives equally well in full sun or light shade and tolerates drought but benefits from occasional waterings during the Summer.

It forms good ornamental ground cover when planted in groups or combined with other shrubs and evergreens. It should be planted at a density of 2 per m.sq. and is suitable for containers. It is propagated from woody cuttings during the Summer.

SP. Tobira enano, Azarero enano FR. - GER. - IT.: *Pittosporum tobira* 'nana'

148. *POLYGALA MYRTIFOLIA*

S.Africa - M -  - IV/X - - (-7°C.) -

Milkwort, Sweet-pea shrub

A graceful shrub with a long flowering period. It is rounded and dense and suitable for ground cover . It grows up to 1.2 m. with dark green foliage similar to that of myrtle and abundant, glossy mauve or purple, butterfly-like flowers in terminal racemes. It is drought resistant but benefits from fresh soil. A sun lover which tolerates partial shade but flowers with less vigour. It naturalizes freely. The '*grandiflora*' variety in the photograph has larger flowers and leaves but is lower growing (90 cm.).

Very useful on slopes and rockeries and as a long-lasting flowering bed combined with *Hypericum, Helichrysum, Artemisia, Cineraria,* and *Chrysanthemum.* Suitable for containers. An annual pruning in March maintains compactness. This disease-free plant is propagated from lateral-shoot cuttings in April.

SP. Lechera del Cabo, Amariposada FR. Faux buis   GER. - IT.: *Polygala myrtifolia*

149. *POLYGONUM CAPITATUM*

N.India - R -  - VI/VIII - — - (-9°C.) -

Knot-weed, Ground Polygonum, Pink fleece-flower

Vigorous carpeter best grown in mild areas as the leaves die back at the first hint of frost. It can become invasive. It reaches 10 cm. tall and has small, decorative leaves and pretty pink flowers.

It will tolerate drought if watered occasionally although moist clay soils are best. It is recommended as cover for small and medium areas planted at a density of 4 per m.sq. It is easily propagated by division in October or March and combines well with *Ajuga, Bacopa, Brachycome, Campanula, Centraderia, Lysimachia congestiflora, Saxifraga, Tradescantia, Viola hederacea* etc.

SP. Nudosilla GER. Knöterich   FR. - IT.: *Polygonum capitatum*

150. *POLYPODIUM VULGARE*

Europe - L -   [!] TOLERA LA CAL

Adder's fern

Highly ornamental, rustic fern with creeping, fleshy rhizomes and persistent fronds some 30 cm. long, segmented in two parallel rows. In Winter the leaf-segments point upwards showing the mature sporangia on their undersides. Grows in almost any soil even calcareous ones as long as they are humus-rich and it is drought resistant.

Ideal cover under trees, on shaded rockeries and partially shaded, shallow, stony ground. It is suitable for pots and is propagated by rhizome division in April when small pieces should be planted just below the soil surface. The rhizomes have a sweet taste of licorice and have medicinal properties.

SP. Polipodio, Filipodio FR. Polypode commun GER. Engelsüss, Túpfelfarn

IT. Felce dolce, Polipodio.

151. POURRETIA MEXICANA (*Fascicularia pitcairniifolia*)

Chile - L - ![perenne] ![pleno sol] ![tolera la sombra] ![tolera la cal] - (-3°C.) - ![soporta la proximidad del mar] ![tolera la contaminación del aire]

Pourretia mexicana

Pretty, stemless bromelia with rosettes of coriaceous, curved leaves with spiny borders. The small blue, short-lived flowers grow from the heart of the rosette. During the flowering period and for some months after the central leaf-bases turn a vivid red colour. The main rosette dies after flowering but not before producing various new plantlets from the base which can be left to broaden the cover or separated for propagation of the plant in April.

It is highly resistant to drought and grows in all types of soil. It thrives in full sun but is also an excellent plant for shaded conditions. It is a slow-growing cover plant for small areas and can be attractively placed next to trunks or stones. It is also suitable for pots.

SP. Purretia   FR. - GER. - IT.: *Pourretia mexicana*

152. *PRUNUS LAUROCERASUS* 'Otto Luyken'

Horticultural - L - 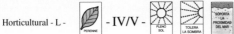 - IV/V -

Cherry bay

Attractive, compact shrub with characteristic, extensive growth. It is a small-sized clone of the European *Prunus laurocerasus* which grows to 90 cm. tall and about 1.8 m. across making it a useful ground-cover plant. The leaves are narrower than the typical form, dark-green, glossy and pointed at the tip. It produces curious spikes of small white flowers in Spring and Autumn if left unpruned. The fruit are small, red and cherry-like changing to black as they mature. It will grow in any deep soil as long as it is not excessively calcareous. It tolerates shade and is ideal for forming low hedges.

It is a useful cover plant grown alone or in groups and should be pruned , if necessary towards the end of the Winter. It is propagated from semi-hard cuttings in August and is toxic as the leaves contain hydrocyanic (prussic)acid.

SP. Lauroceraso, Laurel real FR. Laurier cerise GER. Lobeerkirsche IT. Lauroceraso

153. *RAPHIOLEPIS INDICA* 'Springtime'

Horticulture - M - - IV/V -   - (-9°C.) -

Pink hawthorn

Attractive, dense, brambly shrub with splendid foliage and attractive inflorescences. It grows up to 1.5 m. high and is rounded and neat in form. The dark-green lustrous leaves contrast well with the bronze hues of its tender shoots. The striking, glowing, light pink flowers appear sporadically from February through to August and are followed by long-lasting purple fruits. It prefers fresh, loose soil rich in humus but will grow even in poor soils and it tolerates periods of drought.

Covers the ground alone or in mixed flowerbeds along with *Ceanothus, Diplopappus fruticosus, Euryops, Phylica etc.* It should be maintained low (1m.) by pruning the young shoots after flowering and is propagated from woody cuttings in August. It is suitable for containers.

SP. Manzanillo FR. - GER.- IT. *Raphiolepis indica* 'Springtime'

154. *ROSMARINUS OFFICINALIS*

Mediterranean - M - I/IV -

Rosemary

A jewel of the Mediterranean garden, this erect shrub with aromatic, linear dark-green leaves which have a greyish undersurface produces abundant light blue flowers from January to April. It reflowers every couple of months throughout the year. It loves basic soils but will grow in almost all substrates and is very drought resistant. Amongst the many varieties, 'Pyramidalis' (in the photograph) is the most interesting due to its dense foliage and its potential as a low hedge.

It forms excellent ground cover, forming flowerbeds in dry gardens, on slopes and rockeries. It combines well with groups of *Artemisia, Callistemon, Centaurea, Cineraria, Cistus, Euryops pectinatus, Limoniastrum, Lotus, Malvastrum, Phlomis, Santolina etc.* It requires compacting by pruning in April or May and is propagated from cuttings in October. It repels insects and is both edible and medicinal. It is suitable for use as a pot plant.

SP. Romero FR. Romarin GER. Rosmarin IT. Rosmarino

155. RUSCHIA TUMIDULA (Mesembryanthemum tumidulum)

S. Africa - M - [PERENNE] - V/IX - [PLENO SOL] - [TOLERA LA CAL] - (-5°C.) - [SOPORTA LA PROXIMIDAD DEL MAR] [TOLERA LA CONTAMINACIÓN DEL AIRE]

Ruschia tumidula

Highly interesting, creeping succulent which forms dense, pretty carpets about 5-7 cm. tall and covered with flowers. It tolerates trampling and is extraordinarily resistant to drought.

Very useful as cover for dry, low maintenance areas and grows in all soils including poor, arid or calcareous (or all these three 'virtues' together) and close to the sea. Suitable for small and medium areas. It has the asset of its reddish flowers which are very long-lasting. It is suitable for potting and is propagated freely from cuttings taken in October. Combines well with areas covered with *Gazania, Lippia, Myoporum parvifolium, Nananthus, Sedum, Frankenia, Zoysia, Cerastium etc.*

SP. Esterilla   FR. - GER. - IT.: *Ruschia tumidula*

156. RUSCUS ACULEATUS

Mediterranean - L - IV/V -

Butcher's broom

Erect, expansive shrub some 90 cm. tall with flattened, heart-shaped cladodes. The tiny, unattractive greenish female flowers give rise to abundant bright red fruits during the Autumn which last through the Winter.

Thrives in all soils even, shallow, calcareous or clay ones and tolerates drought and deep shade. It is suitable for containers.

Although slow growing it forms excellent, soil fixing cover for decorating dark areas under trees when planted in groups alongside trunks or stones. It is propagated by division in March. This is a medicinal plant and the fruits are toxic.

SP. Acebillo, Brusco, Rusco FR. Fragon piquant GER. Stechende mäusedorn

IT. Pungitopo.

157. *RUSCUS HYPOGLOSSUM*

Mediterranean - M   - (-9°C.) -

Mouse-thorn

Wide, spreading bush with flexible branches and dense foliage, suitable ground cover. Cladodes large, 6-10 cm. long, without spines. The small flowers are yellow with purple stamens. The scarlet fruit are larger than *R. aculeatus,* some 2 cm. in diameter. It grows in any soils and tolerates full shade.

Ideal cover for shaded areas and dark wooded zones. It is attractive alongside *Polypodium.* It should be planted at a density of 3 per m.sq. and can be used on a large or small scale. It is suitable for containers and is propagated by division in March. The fruit are toxic.

SP .Laurelillo, Bislingua FR. Fragon hypoglosse GER. Mäusedorn

IT. *Ruscus hypoglossum.*

158. *SAGINA SUBULATA (Sagina pilifera)*

S.Europe - R - ![leaf icon PERENNE] - V/VI - ![sun icon PLENO SOL] ![shade icon TOLERA LA SOMBRA]

Pearlwort, Irish or Scotch moss

A pretty, herbaceous plant growing into a dense but subtle, low carpet (5-10 cm. high), formed from linear, bearded leaves. Produces abundant, attractive white flowers. Grows in any fresh soils which are not excessively basic. The 'aurea' form with golden leaves forms very original carpets.

Tolerates moderate trampling and does not require mowing. Useful for carpeting small areas and rock gardens and for filling spaces between flagstones, steps and paved areas. Propagated by direct sowing of seed in Spring and by division in April. It is commercialized in slabs which can be cut up.

SP. Musgosa, Perlada FR. Sagine GER. Mastkraut, Stermoos IT. Sagina

159. SALVIA (GREGGII x MICROPHYLLA)

S.Africa - M - - V/X - - (-9°C.) -

Phylica ericoides

   Compact , low maintenance, ericoid shrub up to 90 cm. tall with a prolonged Winter flowering period. Young shoots are grey and the leaves greyish above with whitish undersides. It produces numerous compact, greyish inflorescence branches with white, button-like flowers. It resists basic soils but prefers neutral to slightly acidic substrates. It adapts to drought and to half-shade.

   It is a useful ground-cover plant for Mediterranean gardens and is highly ornamental when combined with other plants in flowerbeds, on rockeries and slopes. It should be cut down almost to the ground in April followed by a light pruning in June to encourage compact flowering. It is propagated from cuttings taken in July.

SP. Botonera FR. Bruyère du Cap   GER. - IT.: *Phylica ericoides*

160. *SALVIA MICROPHYLLA (Salvia grahamii)*

Mexico - R - ![PERENNE] - V/X - ![PLENO SOL] ![TOLERA LA CAL] - (-9°C.) - ![SOPORTA LA PROXIMIDAD DEL MAR] ![MELIFERA] ![TOLERA LA CONTAMINACIÓN DEL AIRE]

Sage

Vigorous shrub with weak, semi-herbaceous stems which forms a dome shaped mass 75 cm. tall. The small leaves are oval and have a minty aroma. The abundant flowers have a purple cup and carmine corolla which ages to purple. It flowers intermittently throughout the year in mild conditions and grows in any permeable soil. It is drought resistant. The subspecies *microphylla* is less vigorous, growing only to 60 cm. and has dark red flowers. The variety *'neurepia'* grows up to 1 m., has larger, light green leaves and flowers with green cups and reddish-pink corollas. There are other cultivars with pink, orange and magenta flowers.

It is useful when grown as a large ground-covering mass, alternated with *Artemisia, Cineraria, Teucrium etc.* It should be pruned hard in March with two or three cosmetic, light prunings to compact it during the year. It should be planted at 2-3 per m. sq. And is propagated from cuttings taken in Spring. The flowers produce sweet nectar.

SP. Salvia micro FR. Sauge GER. Salbei IT. Salvia.

161. *SALVIA OFFICINALIS (Salvia hispanica)*

S.Europe - M -  - V/VII-

Sage

Branched shrub 60-80 cm. tall with elongated, 5-10 cm. leaves which are grey, velvety and aromatic. The violet-blue flowers grow in abundant, showy racemes. This plant is very resistant to drought and prospers in any, even the most inhospitable, well-drained soil. There are various highly ornamental cultivars: 'ictenna' (in the photograph) with leaves streaked with yellow, 'purpurascens' (photograph) with purple leaves and 'tricolor' variegated with cream, white and pink. These are all more susceptible to disease than the typical form.

All forms are good cover in flowerbeds, rockeries and slopes in dry gardens. It should be planted at 3 per m.sq. Overwatered soil and intense heat are damaging. It can be pruned if necessary, in March with an additional annual pruning after flowering. It is propagated from cuttings in October. This species is suceptible to attack from snails, slugs, greenfly and mites. It is prized as a medicinal herb.

SP. Salvia de Aragón, Salvia real FR. Sauge de Provence GER. Salbei IT. Salvia.

162. *SANTOLINA CHAMAECYPARISSUS*

Mediterranean - R · - V/VII -

Lavender cotton

Compact bush, like a flattened ball, 30-50 cm. tall. Highly ornamental due to its pretty, incised, silver-grey tomentose leaves with apleasant aroma. It produces abundant small, bright, golden-yellow flowers. Thrives in poor, stony, calcareous ground provided that it is well-drained. It is very drought resistant. The variety *nana* grows only to about 20 cm.

Excellent cover planted in groups in dry area gardens, slopes and rockeries. Contrats well when combined with *Rosmarinus* and *Cistus*. It is a good firebreak. T should be pruned severly in Autumn and withered flowers should be removed. It should never be pruned in the Winter. Propagation is from cuttings, tender in June or woody in October. The flowers can be used to repel moths from cupboards and an infusion of flowers is a good insecticide and has medicinal properties.

SP. Santolina, Abrótano, Bocha conejera, Guardarropa FR. Santoline, Petit cyprès GER. Heiligenkraut IT. Santolina.

163. SASA AURICOMA
(Arundinaria auricoma, Arundinaria viridistriata, Pleioblastus viridistriatus 'Auricoma'*)*

Japan - M -

Gold bamboo

Magnificent plant, the brightness of its foliage which is accentuated in Winter and its purplish-green canes make it undoubtedly one of the World's most attractive small bamboos which grows to 80-100 cm. tall. The leaves are slightly velvety, green and glossy and striped with a rich golden-yellow hue. They are often damaged by the strong Summer sun. It prospers in almost any fresh soil and is drought resistant.

It is useful as cover for small areas and is a soil stabilizer. It is of great ornamental value in any composition and is interesting for flowerbeds, woodlands, clearings and rockeries. It is beautiful placed alongside water features. A site should be reserved for it alongside a deciduous tree which provides midday shade. Too much shade, however, dulls the colour. It is easily propagated by division in March or April after its annual pruning. It is suitable for containers.

SP. - FR. - GER. - IT.: *Sasa auricoma*

164. *SASA PUMILA*
(Arundinaria pumila, Pleioblastus pumilus, Pleioblastus humilis)

Japan - R -

Dwarf bamboo

A dwarf species (40-80 cm.) which forms vigorous compact clumps of fine, erect canes, sporting dark green leaves up to 15 cm. long. Excellent ground cover growing in any soil but not particulary resistant to drought. It tolerates direct sun only as long as water is plentiful but prefers, and grows better, in half-shade.

A good ground fixer for fresh slopes due to its rapid growth. An attractive plant for woodlands and next to water or rocks. It should be pruned annually in March before the leaves sprout to maintain it low and compact. A drastic pruning down to ground-level is needed every couple of years. Propagation is by division in March. It is a suitable plant for containers.

SP. - FR. - GER. - IT.: *Sasa pumila.*

165. SASA PYGMAEA
(Arundinaria pygmaea, Arundinaria vagans, Pleioblastus viridistriatus 'Vagans', Sasa ramosa)

Japan - M -

Pygmy bamboo

Small (80-100 cm.) elegant yet rustic bamboo whose rhizomes for excellent cover . Spreads agressively and naturalizes easily. The leaves are pubescent, about 12 cm. long and especially attractive during the Winter due to their beige-white borders. Distinguished from *S. pumila* by its lighter, more flexible leaves. It grows in any soil and tolerates full sun and resists a certain degree of drought although the leaves have a tendancy to curl up in dry conditions.

Useful as a ground fixer in difficult conditions, slopes, forest margins and clearings. The 'variegata' form has white marked leaves. It should be pruned down in March and propagated by division of clumps.

SP. - FR. - GER. - IT.: *Sasa pygmaea.*

165

166. SASA RUSCIFOLIA
(Phyllostachys ruscifolia, Shibataea kumasaca)

China, Japan - M -

Sasa ruscifolia

Often erroneously classified as *Shibataea 'kumasasa'* , this is a small (50-150 cm.) compact, relatively graceful bamboo which has been cultivated in Japan since ancient times. The unique appearance of this species, reminiscent of *Ruscus hypoglossum*, comes from the shape of its leaves. The dense clumps of glossy foliage hide greenish brown zig-zagging canes. It requires fresh soil and light shade. Excess sun is detrimental while the charm of the leaves and plant are lost in full shade.

It is good cover, planted in groups, for semi-shaded areas and is useful for low hedges, either semi-natural or pruned. It is suitable for containers. It requires a light annual pruning in March and is propagated by the division of clumps also in March.

SP. - FR. - GER. - IT.: *Sasa ruscifolia.*

167. *SASA VARIEGATA*
(Arundinaria variegata, Pleioblastus fortunei)

Japan - R -

Miniature bamboo

Attractive, dwarf species (70-90 cm.), rustic and very vigorous. It forms a dense clump as its stems branch close to the base and it extends rapidly. The long velvety leaves are highly decorative and are streaked with creamy-white lines. It grows in all soils but prefers them fresh. It thrives in half-shade but the full beauty of the leaves is best appreciated in full sun.

Best used to create bright patches of vegetation in gardens placing it so that it stands out due to the unique coloration. Useful cover for slopes, rockeries and copses and is very beautiful placed next to water. Recommended as a soil fixer. Suitable for containers, it should be pruned low in Spring and propagated by division in March.

SP. - FR. - GER. - IT.: *Sasa variegata.*

168. *SATUREJA MONTANA*

S.Europe - M -  - V/VII -

Winter savory

A small, aromatic shrub some 30 cm. tall with numerous branches. It is covered with small, dark-green, lanceolate leaves and, in May to June, with small white flowers. It accepts any well-drained soil even if poor, arid, stony or calcareous. It thrives on and resists drought.

Covers the ground in unwatered areas of the garden, on slopes and amongst rocks. In flowerbeds it combines well with other aromatics such as *Lavandula, Rosmarinus, Santolina, Teucrium chamaedrys* and *Thymus*. It is propagated from seed or by October cuttings. An infusion of the leaves is a stimulant and induces appetite as well as having stomachal properties. It can be used as a seasoning for meat and olives. It is a suitable subject for flowerpots.

SP. Ajedrea, Hisopillo FR. Sarriette de montagne GER. Zwerg-bergminze

IT. Santoreggia.

169. SAXIFRAGA SARMENTOSA (Saxifraga stolonifera)

China, Japan - R -  - VII/VIII -

Strawberry geranium

Attractive, stoloniferous, creeping plant with a healthy appearance. Produces long, tender, reddish stems which root as they advance producing new plantlets at their extremities. Does not grow more than 20 cm. high and has pretty, rounded leaves resembling those of geraniums. The graceful inflorescences are made up of small white flowers. Does not grow well in full sun but tolerates any type of soil and partial drought.

Excellent carpeting plant for shaded areas. Useful for small plantings, combining attractively with *Helxine*. It should be planted at a density of 5 per m. sq. 'Tricolor' Is a good variety with pink and white leaf-edges but it is less vigorous and more sensitive to cold and intense shade spoils the coloration. It is suitable for potting and can be propagated by separation plantlets in Spring or Autumn.

SP. Saxífraga china FR. Saxifrage sarmenteuse GER. Judenbart

IT. Sassifraga sarmentosa.

170. *SCAEVOLA HUMILIS (Scaevola aemula)*

Australia - R - [PERENNE] - V/XI - [PLENO SOL] - (-3°C.) - [SOPORTA LA PROXIMIDAD DEL MAR] [TOLERA LA CONTAMINACIÓN DEL AIRE]

Fan flower, Half-flower

An attractive creeping or hanging, semisucculent evergreen with intense, slightly toothed leaves. It is fast-growing forming cushions about 20-25 cm. high. It produces curious, violet- blue flowers with 5, fan-shaped petals. Accepts any substantial, permeable soil and benefits from dry conditions. It prospers in full sun but also flowers extraordinarily well in semi-shade and the extensive flowering period can last, in frost-free conditions, until December.

Excellent floral cover for rockeries and small, dry areas. Excessive humidity can be fatal. It makes a good pot subject and is easily propagated from cuttings taken in Spring.

SP. Abanico, Escévola   FR. - GER. - IT.: *Scaevola humilis*

171. *SEDUM CAUTICOLUM* 'Lidakense'

Horticulture (Japan)- R -  - VIII/X -

Orpine

   Low, compact, prostrate succulent with purple extremities, reaching a height of 15 cm.. The leaves are 3 cm. long , rounded and incised, blue-green with a reddish tinge. The pretty flowers are bright pink. It will grow in full sun and any soil.

   Provides low maintenance cover for largeand small areas and is ideal for dry ground, slopes and rockeries as well as for pots. It is a beautiful subject, at its best in Autumn. It is freely proagated from cuttings in Autumn.

SP. *Sedum* FR. Orpin GER. Fetthenne IT. *Sedum.*

172. *SEDUM KAMTSCHATICUM*

E.Asia - R -  - VI/IX -

Stone-crop

   Pretty carpeting succulent forming a dense mass up to 15 cm. high. The leaves are flat, spathulate and incised, 3-5 cm. long and tender green in colour. It produces numerous, lightly perfumed yellow flowers with orange centres throughout the Summer.
   Grows in full sun and in any soil and is fast growing. Good carpeter for small and large areas in dry gardens, slopes and rocky terrain. It is apt for pots and is propagated from cuttings taken in April.

SP. *Sedum* FR. Orpin GER. Fetthenne IT. *Sedum.*

173. *SEDUM PACHYPHYLLUM*

Mexico - M -  PERENNE - III/IV - PLENO SOL - TOLERA LA CAL - (-3°C.) - SOPORTA LA PROXIMIDAD DEL MAR - TOLERA LA CONTAMINACIÓN DEL AIRE

Jelly beans

Erect but compact succulent with cylindrical, curved, blue-green leaves, 3-4 cm. long with red tips. Grows to 20-25 cm. The flowers are light yellow and come in small, dense clusters. It thrives in any soil and in full sun.

It provides elegant cover for small areas in dry, rocky gardens and is suitable for potting. It is freely propagated from cuttings taken in May.

SP. *Sedum* FR. Orpin GER. Fetthenne IT. *Sedum.*

174. SEDUM PALMERI

Mexico - R -  - II/III - ☀ PLENO SOL - ! TOLERA LA CAL - (-9°C.) - SOPORTA LA PROXIMIDAD DEL MAR - ✓ TOLERA LA CONTAMINACIÓN DEL AIRE

Orpine

Interesting, attractive, fast-growing cover, reaching a height of only 10–15 cm. It has flat, fleshy sea-green leaves which form rosettes. It flowers early and has pretty, yellow-orange, lateral flowers.

It thrives on any permeable soil even if calcareous. It generally requires full sun but will tolerate half-shade during the Summer. It is ideal, low maintenance cover for both small and large areas surviving without irrigation. It is also suitable for containers and is easily propagated from April cuttings.

SP. *Sedum* FR. Orpin GER. Fetthenne IT. *Sedum.*

175. SEDUM PRAEALTUM

Mexico - R -  - II/IV -

Orpine

Often erroneously found under the name *Sedum dendroideum,* this is a large, compact succulent growing to 1.5 m. if left unpruned. The spathulate, curved leaves are 5-7 cm. long and are glossy yellow-green, tinged with bronze and grow in rosettes at the tips of the stems. The attractive flowers are bright yellow and appear as tall inflorescences in Winter and through Spring..

It is suitable for covering shrubberies and flowerbeds and areas of dry garden, slopes and rockeries. It can also be used as an untrained, almost impenetrable hedge. It loves full sun and any soil, even calcareous or exposed to the sea. It can be alternated with Winter-flowering shrubs such as *Diplopappus, Eriocephalus, Phylica , Rosmarinus etc.* It is suitable for containers and is propagated from cuttings taken in May. It should be lightly pruned in the same month.

SP. *Sedum* FR. Orpin GER. Fatthenne IT. *Sedum*

176. *SEDUM x RUBROTINCTUM*

Mexico - M - [PERENNE] - IV/V - [PLENO SOL] - [TOLERA LA CAL] - (-3°C.) - [SOPORTA LA PROXIMIDAD DEL MAR] - [TOLERA LA CONTAMINACIÓN DEL AIRE]

Christmas cheer

Small, yet highly decorative creeping succulent some 20 cm. tall. The leaves are wedge shaped, 2 cm. long and bright glossy green becoming tinged with a pretty bronze-red in the Summer. The flowers are bright yellow and the 'aurora' variety has grey-green leaves tinged with dark red. This plant prospers in any soil and in full sun.

It is good ground cover for small areas in arid gardens slopes and rockeries. It is attractive placed alongside rocks and trunks. It is suitable for potting and is easily propagated from cuttings taken after flowering.

SP. *Sedum* FR. Orpin GER. Fetthenne IT. *Sedum.*

177. *SEDUM SPURIUM* 'Tricolor'

Horticulture (Caucasus) - R - 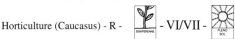 - VI/VII -

Stone crop

Low (only 10 cm. high) carpeting succulent with rosettes of flat, rounded , 2.5 cm. across, reddish-pink streaked, toothed leaves variegated with white. It has delicate, reddish pink flowers during the Summer. It accepts all types of soil but requires full sun to maintain its attractive colouring.

Useful for covering small and medium areas with masses of rich colour, contrasting vividly with the green of other plants. Combines well with *Sedum kantschaticum* and is suitable for use as a pot plant. It is freely propagated from cuttings which are best taken in March.

SP. *Sedum* FR. Orpin GER. Fettehenne IT. *Sedum.*

178. SENECIO LEUCOSTACHYS
(Cineraria candidissima, Senecio vira-vira)

Patagonia - M -  - IV/VI -   - (-9°C.) -

Senecio leucostachys

Highly decorative species with shiny, silver to almost white foliage. A vigorous, lax shrub which forms a mass of incised, tomentose, silvery leaves and corymbs of yellow flowers which appear toward the end of the Spring. It grows to about 70 cm. high and accepts all types of soil. It is drought resistant. This plant is useful as its whiteness brightens up the garden even at night.

Useful for covering ground in unwatered gardens and combines perfectly with groups of *Ceanothus, Cistus, Cuphea micropetala, Lobelia laxiflora, Rosmarinus, Salvia microphylla etc.* It should be planted at a density of 3 per m.sq. and is suitable for containers. It is propagated from lateral, semi-woody cuttings taken during the Summer.

SP. Fúlgida, Viravira   FR. - GER.- IT.: *Senecio leucostachys*

179. SENECIO MIKANIOIDES
(Delairea odorata, Mikania scandens)

S.Africa - R - [PERENNE] VI/XI - [FLOR PERFUMADA] [PLENO SOL] [TOLERA LA SOMBRA] [TOLERA LA CAL] - (-3°C.) - [SOPORTA LA PROXIMIDAD DEL MAR] [TOLERA LA CONTAMINACIÓN DEL AIRE]

German ivy, Parlour ivy, Canary creeper

Vigorous invasive shrub with herbaceous, vine-like stems which can climb, hang or creep along the ground. It forms excellent cover and is a good climber despite its fragile appearance. The stems reach lengths of 6-7 m. and it is a plant which naturalizes easily in Mediterranean areas. Highly appropriate as ground cover as the stems root at the nodes as they extend. It resists drought and tolerates all soil types without any particular preferences. The heart-shaped, somewhat fleshy, tender green, glossy leaves are about 5 cm.long and have 3-7 lobes closely resembling ivy. It produces abundant, long-lasting, pale-yellow flowers and grows well in half-shade but flowers best in full sun. It is suitable for containers and is useful for covering small or large surfaces. It is propagated by planting cuttings directly *in situ*, these rooting freely in the Spring.

SP. Mikania, Hiedra alemana FR. Séneçon mikanie GER.- IT.: *Senecio mikanioides.*

180. *SENECIO PETASITIS*
(Senecio platanifolius, Cineraria petasites)

S.W.Mexico - R  - I/III - 🌞 ⛅ ⚠ - (-3°C.) - 🏖

Velvet groundsel, California geranium.

Magnificent, rounded, branched shrub, 90-150 cm. high which forms an attractive mass of foliage, structurally impressive and with a tropical air. The leaves are large, rounded and velvety and turn reddish in cold weather. The glossy yellow flowers grow in large terminal panicles during the Winter. The stems and leaves are lost at –4°C. but the plant will survive lower temperatures down to –11°C. sprouting anew in Spring. It accepts all types of soil and tolerates drought.

The large, contrasting leaves make this a highly decorative species. It can be planted alone or in groups and is very pretty placed close to water. Flowering can be suppressed to compact the foliage. Pruning should be done in April to improve density and produce larger leaves. It is propagated by semi-woody cuttings taken in April and is disease resistant.

SP. Plantanillo

FR. - GER. - IT.: *Senecio petasites*

181. *SENECIO SAXIFRAGA*

Argentina - R -  - IV/IX - [PLENO SOL] [TOLERA LA SOMBRA] [! TOLERA LA CAL] - (-5°C.) - [SOPORTA LA PROXIMIDAD DEL MAR] [TOLERA LA CONTAMINACIÓN DEL AIRE]

Senecio saxifraga

Often wrongly named as *Senecio doronicum 'hosmariensis',* this small, graceful, herbaceous plant which grows to 20-30 cm. tall is vigorous and highly floriferous. It small, glossy,light-green, incised leaves are reminiscent of those of *Campanula muralis.* The small flowers are golden-yellow and starlike. Grows in any rich and well-drained soil. Tolerates a certain degree of drought but requires periodic watering. Adapts well to half-shade where it can be pleasantly combined with the similar *Campanula* and many other evergreen shrubs as ornamental ground-covering. It flowers best in full sun and is ideal for rockeries and mixed borders where it attracts butterflies. It is propagated by division in Spring or Autumn.

SP. Campánula amarilla   FR. - GER. - IT.: *Senecio saxifraga*

182. STACHYS LANATA

(Stachys byzantina, Stachys olympica)

Turkey - R - 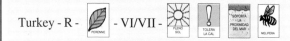 - VI/VII -

Lamb's ears

Attractive perennial forming a clump (10-20 cm.high) of large leaves covered with a white silky felt. The leaves may partially dry out in Winter. Produces tall (50-70 cm.) spikes of violet-pink flowers. Resists drought and is content in any soil.

Unique covering for small areas, mixed borders, slopes and rockeries. It should be planted at 5 per m.sq. and combines elegantly with many other species. The leaves are protected from parasites by their woolly coating. Suitable for containers and propagated by seed sown in Autumn or by division in March and April.

SP. Lanuda, Orejas de liebre FR. Oreilles d'ours GER. Wollzeist IT. *Stachys lanata.*

183. *STENOTAPHRUM GLABRUM*
(Stenotaphrum americanum, Stenotaphrum secundatum)

American tropics - R -  (-7°C.) -

Buffalo grass, St. Augustine grass

A robust, mowable grass mentioned here because of the 'variegatum' form which is suitable for covering small surfaces that do not need mowing. A pretty, vigorous grass with flat, laminar, erect leaves variegated with cream which grow up to 15 cm. in height.

Adapts to all soil types even sandy and calcareous and requires only occasional waterings and withstands intense trampling.   The leaves fade to a straw-colour if the temperature drops below freezing but survive well in areas protected from frost.

Useful for covering difficult corners where most other plants will not grow. It requires periodic pruning and can be freely propagated in April or May from stolon cuttings. The species is cultivated for forage.

SP. Gramón, cañamazo, grama americana FR. Chiendent de boeuf GER. Buffalogras IT. *Stenotaphrum glabrum.*

184. *TEUCRIUM CHAMAEDRYS*

S. Europe - L - [PERENNE] - V/IX - [PLENO SOL] [TOLERA LA SOMBRA] [! TOLERA LA CAL] [MELIFERA]

Germander

Small, but extensive bush some 30 cm. high with small glossy, indented, dark green leaves which are aromatic when crushed. It produces abundant pink flowers throughout the Summer and there is a dwarf form which only grows to 20 cm.

Tolerates poor, arid soils and is useful for covering large or small areas in dry gardens, rockeries and slopes. It can be planted with other aromatics such as *Lavandula, Rosmarinus, Santolina, Thymus etc.* It is propagated from cuttings in October and is suitable for potting. It also has medicinal properties.

SP. Camedrio, Encinilla FR. Cheênette GER. Gamander IT. Querciòla, calandrea.

185. *TEUCRIUM FRUTICANS (Teucrium tomentosum)*

W. Mediterranean - M - - II-VI -   - (-9°C.)

Bush germander

Shrub with spreading whitish branches forming a compact mass of pretty foliage. The small smooth leaves are greyish on top with whitish, tomentose undersides. It produces abundant pale blue flowers in pairs at the base of the leaves. It resists pruning well making it a good subject for low hedges. The attractive 'compactum' variety is very dense whilst the 'azureum' form has more intensely coloured blue flowers but is sensitive to the cold.

Good for covering flowerbeds, slopes and rock gardens producing contrasting effects due to its colour. Resists drought well. It should be planted at 1 per m.sq. and is suitable for containers. Shoot tips should be removed regularly to maintain density and it can be pruned at any time. It is propagated from cuttings which should be taken in October.

SP. Olivillo, Teucrio FR. Germandrée arbustive Ger. Gamander IT. Teucrio.

186. *THYMUS SERPYLLUM*
(Thymus angustifolius, Thymus pulegioides)

Europe - R - 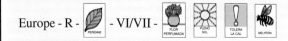 - VI/VII -

Creeping thyme, Mother-of-thyme

Shrublet, some 25 cm. tall, prostrate and spreading with erect tips. Small dark green leaves and pink flowers during the Summer. Tolerates drought and grows in poor arid soil.

Excellent covering, especially for dry, stony terrain. Useful for both large and small areas. Should be planted at a density of 6 per m. sq. The cultivar'coccineus' with crimson (VI/VIII) flowers only grows about 10 cm. high forming magnificent carpets which are moderately resistant to trampling. Combines well with *Agathaea, Brachycome, Cerastium, Dianthus, Erigeron, Felicia, Festuca, Nepeta, Santolina, Satureja, Sedum kamptschaticum, Verbena tenera etc.* It is propagated from Spring or Autumn cuttings and has medicinal properties.

SP. Serpol FR. Serpolet, Thym serpolet, GER. Feldthymian IT. Serpillo, Serpolo.

187. *THYMUS VULGARIS*

Mediterranean Basin - M -  - V/VI -

Thyme

   Small, branched, prostrate shrublet with highly aromatic green leaves. Reaches a height of 25 cm. and produces abundant lilac-red flowers. Grows in all soil types and is highly resistant to drought. Will spontaneously colonise slopes and eroded areas. Excellent coverer of rockeries and stony gardens. A form with grey leaves and a compact form are worth mentioning along with 'argentatus' which is a pretty but slow growing cultivar with variegated leaves. A similar species *Thymus x citriodorus* which is lemon-scented, has a golden variety 'aureus' and another silvery white form ('silver queen'). It is a good pot plant.

   The aroma repels damaging insects. It is a medicinal and seasoning herb which is multiplied from cuttings taken in October.

SP. Tomillo FR. Farigoule GER. Thymian IT. Timo.

188. *TRADESCANTIA x ANDERSONIANA* 'Leonora'

Horticulture USA - R - 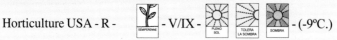 - V/IX - - (-9°C.)

Showy spiderwort, widow's tears

    Despite its delicate appearance, this is a robust perennial with erect stems which forms dense covering but does not suffocate weeds. It reaches a height of 30 cm and produces small but pretty 3-petalled violet flowers. It thrives in all fresh, well-drained soils and will tolerate drought, although regular watering is beneficial. The leaves wither with the first frost and reappear in the Spring.

    It is suitable for covering small surfaces , alternated with *Bacopa, Centradenia, Lamium, Lysimachia, Saxifraga etc.* Plants should be divided every 4-5 years and it is easily propagated from Spring cuttings. The young shoots are favourites of slugs.

SP.Efímera, pasajera FR.Éphémère de Virginie GER. Dreimasterblume IT.Tradescanzia

189. *TRADESCANTIA PALLIDA*
'Purple Heart' *(Setcreasea Purpurea)*

Horticulture (Mexico) - F  - VIII/X - ... - (-3°C.) - ...

Purple heart

Strikingly coloured perennial, which creeps or hangs and grows to about 35 cm. tall. It has large, violet leaves 10-15 cm. long. The violet-pink flowers appear towards the end of Summer. It grows in any soil even calcareous and tolerates drought.

Excellent coverer of small areas, wet or dry, sunny or in shade, and combines well with a multitude of other species, especially those with grey foliage: *Cerastium, Artemisia Centaurea, Eriocephalus, Santolina etc.* and others with yellow flowers. It is a suitable pot subject and can be propagated from cuttings taken from Spring through to Autumn.

SP. Purpurina FR. Éphémère GER. Ampelkraut IT. Miseria viola.

190. *TRADESCANTIA VIRIDIS (Tradescantia albiflora)*

C.America - R -    - (-3°C.) -

Spiderwort

Common, creeping or hanging, herbaceous plant which will climb if provided with support. It has small green leaves and tiny white flowers which appear only rarely. There are varieties with the leaves striped with white, yellow and violet.

Fast carpeter for all fresh, humid or shaded surfaces and will share terrain with *Helxine, Saxifraga* and *Viola*. Suitable for potting and easily propagated from cuttings taken from April through to October.

SP. Miseria FR. Éphémère GER. Wasserranke IT. Erba ragno

191. TRADESCANTIA ZEBRINA (Zebrina pendula)

Mexico - R - - VI/IX- [icons: TOLERA LA SOMBRA | TOLERA LA CAL | TOLERA LA CONTAMINACIÓN DEL AIRE]

Inch plant, Wandering jew

Popular and attractive pot plant which is also very useful for covering ground due to its creeping and hanging habit. It has pretty silvery leaves with purple undersides and small, delicate re-pink flowers which appear during the Summer. It prefers humid soils but will tolerate occasional drought in shaded conditions. It is not fussy about soil type.

Useful for forming graceful carpets, small or medium-sized, under trees or shrubs and can be contrasted elegantly with other green creepers. Propagation from cuttings is child's play.

SP.Zebrina FR. Misère GER. Wasserranke IT. Zebrina

192. TRITOMA UVARIA (Kniphofia uvaria)

S.Africa - R - [PERENNE] - VII - [PLENO SOL] [TOLERA LA CAL] - (-7°C.) - [SOPORTA LA PROXIMIDAD DEL MAR] [MELIFERA] [TOLERA LA CONTAMINACIÓN DEL AIRE]

Torch lily, Red-hot-poker

Forms strong, herbaceous, rhizomatous clumps with stunning flowers. The dark-green ,channelled leaves are erect at first, then curved later. The notable conical spikes of bright orange flowers are borne on long stems. 'Geant', the variety in the photo. Can reach over 2 m. in height. The flowering stems resemble flaming torches. Resists drought but appreciates the occasional Summer watering. Grows in any permeable soil and numerous forms and hybrids exist.

Highly appreciated for covering dry ground, slopes and rock gardens. It is attractive when placed close to water or against a blue background of sky or sea. Combines ornamentally with *Agapanthus, Artemisia, Centaurea pulcherrima, Cineraria, Echium, Gaura, Hypericum, Lavandula, Melianthus, Nepeta, Perovskia, Salvia, Senecio leucostachys etc.* Should be planted at a density of 3 per m.sq. The old flower-spikes should be pruned out from the base to prolong flowering. Large clumps should be divided every 4-5 years to maintain a high level of flowering. Propagation is by division in April.

SP. Tritoma FR. - GER. - IT.: *Tritoma uvaria.*

193. *TROPAEOLUM MAJUS*

S.America - R -  - IV/X - - (-1°C.)

Nasturtium

Vigorous, decorative, herbaceous perennial which must be grown as an annual in areas prone to frost. During the long flowering season it produces brillant yellow or orange flowers. It creeps along the ground with 2-3 m. stems and can also climb or hang. It appreciates fresh, fertile soils that are not too basic. There are numerous dwarf forms and a beautiful variegated form with yellow markings (in the photo.) which can, unusually, be propagated from seed.

Excellent covering for small areas. Excess shade inhibits flowering and dulls the colours of the foliage. It is suitable for pots and is a multi-use plant, the leaves are eaten in salads, the flowers used as a dressing whilst the buds and pea-size seeds contain mustard oil and are eaten in pickles as an alternative to capers. The leaves are eaten by caterpillars and the seeds by birds. It is propagated by seed sown in April.

SP. Capuchina, Espuela de galán, Marañuelas, Pelón Fr. Capucine

GER. Kapuzinerblume, Kapuzinerkresse IT. Astruzia, Cappuccina.

194. *VERBENA x HYBRIDA (Verbena x hortensis)*

Horticulture (C. & S.América) - R - V/XI -   - (-7°C.) -

Garden verbena

Very popular creeping or hanging plant which flowers without interruption throughout the Summer until the first frosts. It forms perfect carpets as the stems fix the soil as they spread. Two types can be distinguished, those that grow erect (30-50 cm-tall) and those which are prostrate and are better carpeters; these are known as 'repens'. Both types have numerous varieties of diverse coloured flowers, red,white, pink, blue etc. It accepts any well-drained soil and tolerates drought.

Useful as profusely flowering covering for small and large surfaces, it can act as a fire-break. It should be planted at 3-5 per m. sq. Depending on the variety and withered flowers should be removed periodically. It ages rapidly and should be replaced every 3-4 years. Propagation is by cuttings in October. Excessive humidity causes mildew and grey mould. This is a good butterfly and hawk-moth plant . The photo. shows 'Cleopatra' a beautiful, fast-growing, erect form with a long flowering period .

SP. Verbena FR. Verveine des jardins GER. Gartenverbene IT. Verbena.

195. *VERBENA TENERA*
(Verbena pulchella, Verbena sellowiana)

S.Brazil, Argentina - R - 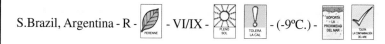 - VI/IX - - (-9°C.) -

Sand vervain

Vigorous, creeping plant with carpeting habit, fast-growing and with a long flowering season. It has finely divided leaves and violet-pink flowers. It prospers in all soils and tolerates drought, benefitting, however, from occasional waterings. It tolerates a certain degree of shade and light trampling. It is useful for carpeting small and large areas and as a firebreak. It should be planted at 3 per m.sq. 'Albiflora' has pure white flowers and var. 'maonettii' has attractive flowers bordered in white.

This species has a useful life of 4-5 years requiring replacement by cuttings planted directly into the soil in October or April.

SP. Verbena repens FR. Verveine GER. Eisenkraut IT. Verbena.

196. VINCA MINOR

Europe - R - PERENNE - IV/V - TOLERA LA SOMBRA SOMBRA TOLERA LA CAL

Dwarf periwinkle, Lesser periwinkle

Vine-like perennial some 15 cm. tall, forming a low, dense carpet useful for covering shady areas. It has long, glossy, dark green leaves and pretty, bright, blue-violet flowers which appear during the Spring. The stems root at the nodes as they spread.

Excellent covering for fresh soil, tolerates drought if watered occasionally. Will prevent the advance of fire if planted en masse. There are various bright varieties, 'argenteovariegata' streaked with white, and 'aureovariegata' with yellow. An annual Spring cut-back is beneficial and it is easily propagated using the already rooted stems. SP. Brusela, Perivinca FR. Petit pervenche GER. Immergrün IT. Pervinca.

197. *VIOLA HEDERACEA*

(Viola reniformis, Erpetion reniforme)

Australia - R -  - VII/IX - [TOLERA LA SOMBRA] [SOMBRA] [! TOLERA LA CAL] - (-7°C.) - [TOLERA LA CONTAMINACIÓN DEL AIRE]

Australian violet, Trailing violet

Small plant with attractive leaves and flowers. An excellent carpeter for shaded areas. A perennial evergreen with vertical rhizomes and long stolons covered with fresh green, rounded leaves, more or less kidney-shaped and some 3 cm. across. In Autumn and occasionaly in Spring it produces abundant white flowers 2 cm. across and with violet-blue striped interior. This species accepts any type of fresh, well drained, healthy soil but requires a shady site.

Forms a beautiful, dense carpet 5-7 cm. thick and will also hang. Good covering for small or medium areas, humid rockeries and under trees etc. Plantings should be at 3 per m. sq. There is a variety with white flowers and another, 'baby blue' with blue flowers. It is propagated by division in Spring or Autumn.

SP. Riñoncillo, Violeta australiana FR. Violette à feuille de lierre GER. Veilchen IT. Viola.

198. *VIOLA ODORATA*

Europe - M -  - III/IV -

Common violet, Sweet violet

Rhizomatous species which extends via stolons and which forms good covering in shaded conditions. It reaches a height of 10-15 cm. and has heart-shaped, darkish green leaves and highly perfumed violet or white flowers some 2 cm. across. These appear in March, or sometimes earlier, in February.

Good covering for small, humid areas although it will tolerate occasional periods of drought. It is suitable for use as a pot plant and there are numerous varieties. It is usually propagated from seed in Autumn or from stolon division in October or March. It is a medicinal plant which is also used in the manufacture of perfume and liqueurs.

SP. Violeta de olor, Violeta dulce FR. Violette, violette de mars

GER. Frühlingsveilchen IT. Viola mammola.

199. WESTRINGIA FRUTICOSA
(Westringia rosmariniformis)

Australia - M - [PERENNE] - V/VII - [PLENO SOL] - (-7°C.) - [SOPORTA LA PROXIMIDAD DEL MAR]

Coast rosemary

Large shrub up to 1.5 m. tall, dense and rounded, resembling rosemary in appearance and texture. Does not spread but remains compact. The leaves are linear, 1-3 cm. long with whitish undersides. The white or pale blue, lipped flowers appear during the Spring and Summer (from February in mild conditions). It is relatively fast-growing but sensitive to excess humidity, requiring perfect drainage. It is resistant to drought and appreciates slightly acidic soils.

Useful for covering the ground in dry gardens, rockeries and sloping surfaces and will grow in close proximity to the sea. Very attractive alongside *Lavandula, Coronilla, Cistus, Diplopappus, Echium, Grevillea, Polygala* and *Salvia microphylla*. Useful as a cut flower and for low hedges. It is propagated from October cuttings.

SP. Romerino   FR .- GER. - IT.: *Westringia fruticosa*

200. *ZOYSIA TENUIFOLIA*

Mauritius, Reunion - L -   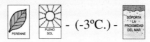   - (-3°C.) -

Korean grass, Mascarense grass

   Caespitose perennial grass with very fine, abundant stolons forming a handsome carpet which is dense, resistant and tolerant of trampling. It does not require regular mowing. It grows to 10 cm. (5 cm. if trmpled) and has long, linear leaves about 1 mm. Thick. It is very slow-growing and tolerates drought but benefits from periodic waterings every 15 days or so during hot weather. A twice yearly mowing in April and October improves ita appearance. It turns yellow during the Winter if temperatures reach –4°C. but it survives down to –12°C. and greens up in the Spring. It is a good alternative to other classical grass species in lawns for large and small areas. It can be established by planting rooted clumps (7 per m.sq.) or from cuttings in Spring and Autumn which root in 2 or 3 weeks. Sold commercially in turf slabs which can be used directly or divided up for planting a larger area.

SP. Isleña, Japonesa FR. Gazon des mascareignes   GER. - IT.: *Zoysia tenuifolia*